20,57

THE BETRAYAL OF THE SOUL
IN PSYCHOTHERAPY

THE BETRAYAL OF THE SOUL IN PSYCHOTHERAPY

(formerly titled **Incest and Human Love**)

ROBERT STEIN

with a foreword by John Ryan Haule

Spring Journal Books, Inc.
Woodstock, Connecticut

The Betrayal of the Soul in Psychotherapy was originally published as *Incest in Human Love* © 1973 by Robert Stein. All rights reserved
"Introduction to the Second Edition" © 1984 by Robert Stein
All rights reserved
"Foreword" by John Ryan Haule © 1998 by Spring Journal Inc.
All rights reserved
First Spring Journal Edition printing 1998

Published by Spring Journal, Inc.: 299 East Quassett Road;
Woodstock, Connecticut 06281
Printed in Canada
Text printed on acidfree paper
Cover production by Audrey Borowski and Marshall Pahl

First published in 1973 by The Third Press,
Joseph Okpaku Publishing Co., Inc., New York
Published in 1974 by Penguin Books Inc., Baltimore, Maryland
Published in 1984 by Spring Publications, Inc., Dallas, Texas

Library in Congress Cataloging in Publication Data
Stein, Robert, 1924–1996
Incest and human love.

(The Jungian classics series)
Reprint. Originally published: New York, N.Y.:
Third Press, c1973. With new introd.
Includes bibliographical references and index.
1. Incest. 2. Sex (Psychology) 3. Love.
4. Psychotherapy. I. Title. II. Series.
RC560.I53S74   1984   150.19'54   83–20465
ISBN 1–882670–16–7 (pbk.)

To
My wife and all
Those patients and friends
Who have shared
In my quest
To heal the soul's
Deep, deep wounds.

Acknowledgments

For the use of copyrighted material grateful acknowledgment is made to the following:

Sigmund Freud Copyrights Ltd., The Institute of Psycho-Analysis, and The Hogarth Press Ltd. for permission to use material from *The Standard Edition of the Complete Psychological Works of Sigmund Freud,* revised and edited by James Strachey;

W.W. Norton & Company, Inc. for permission to use excerpts from the following books: *An Outline of Psycho-Analysis* by Sigmund Freud. Translated by James Strachey. Copyright © 1949 by W.W. Norton & Company, Inc. Copyright © 1969 by The Institute of Psychoanalysis and Alix Strachey; *The Ego And The Id* by Sigmund Freud. Translated by Joan Riviere. Revised and edited by James Strachey. Copyright © 1960 by James Strachey. W.W. Norton & Company, Inc.;

Basic Books, Inc., for permission to use excerpts from the following titles: "The Passing of the Oedipus Complex," *Collected Papers of Sigmund Freud, Vol. 2*; "Instincts and their Vicissitudes," *Collected Papers of Sigmund Freud, Vol. 4;* "The Most Prevalent Form of Degradation in Erotic Life," *Collected Papers of Sigmund Freud, Vol. 4.* Edited by Ernest Jones. Published by Basic Books, Inc. by arrangement with The Hogarth Press Ltd. and The Institute of Psycho-Analysis, London;

Liveright Publishers, New York, for permission to use excerpts from *Beyond the Pleasure Principle* by Sigmund Freud. Copyright © 1961 by James Strachey;

The World Publishing Company, for permission to reprint an excerpt from *On Love* by Jose Ortega y Gasset. Copyright © 1957 by The World Publishing Company. A Meridian Book;

Princeton University Press, for excerpts from the following titles:

Papers from the Eranos Yearbooks, ed. by Joseph Campbell, Bollingen Series XXX, vol. 2, *The Mysteries* trans. by Ralph Manheim (copyright © 1955 by Bollingen Foundation), reprinted by permission of Princeton University Press;

The Collected Works of C. G. Jung, ed. by G. Adler, M. Fordham, W. McGuire and H. Read, trans. by R. F. C. Hull, Bollingen Series XX, vol. *8, The Structure and Dynamics of the Psyche* (copyright © 1960 by Bollingen Foundation and © 1969 by Princeton University Press); reprinted by permission of Princeton University Press; also, from vol. 14, *Mysterium Coniunctionis (*copyright © 1963 by Bollingen Foundation and © 1970 by Princeton University Press; reprinted by permission of Princeton University Press;

ACKNOWLEDGMENTS

Essays on a Science of Mythology, by C. G. Jung and C. Kerényi, trans. by R. F. C. Hull, Bollingen Series XXII (copyright © 1949, 1959, 1963 by Bollingen Foundation); reprinted by permission of Princeton University Press;

Harcourt Brace Jovanovich, Inc. for excerpts from *The Sexual Life of Savages* by Bronislaw Malinowski, published by Harcourt Brace Jovanovich and reprinted by permission of the publishers;

Dover Publications, for an excerpt from *Beyond Psychology* by Otto Rank, New York, Dover Publications, 1958;

Simon & Schuster, Inc. for an excerpt from *The Last Temptation of Christ* by N. Kazantzakis, copyright © 1960 by Simon & Schuster, Inc. Reprinted by permission of the publishers;

Grove Press, Inc. for excerpts from: *The Heroes of the Greeks* by C. Kerènyi, New York, Grove Press, 1960, and *Lady Charterley's Lover* by D.H. Lawrence, New York, Grove Press. Introduction by Mark Schorer copyright © 1957 by Grove Press, Inc. Letter from Archibald MacLeish © 1959 by Grove Press, Inc. Reprinted by permission of the publishers.

Random House, Inc. for an excerpt from *Ego and Instinct*, 1970 by D. Yankelovich and W. Barrett © 1970 by Yankelovich & Barrett. Reprinted by permission of Random House, Inc.

Twayne Publishers, Inc. for an excerpt from "A Propos of Lady Chatterley's Lover" by D. H. Lawrence in *Sex, Literature, and Censorship,* edited by Harry T. Moore, New York, Twayne Publishers, 1953. Reprinted by permission of the publishers.

Horizon Press, for permission to use excerpts from "Love of God and Love of Neighbor," in *Hasidism and Modern Man* by Martin Buber, © 1958.

S. Karger, Basel, for permission to use excerpts from "Der Archetyp" in *Ueber religiose Hintergrunde des Puer-Aeternus-Problems.* Verh. 2. int. Kongr, analyt. Psychol., Zürich 1962, 141-156. (Karger AG, Basel 1964)

Humanities Press, Inc., New York, for permission to use excerpts from *Sex and Repression in Savage Society,* by Bronislaw Malinowski.

The material on viii is from *The Basic Writings of Sigmund Freud,* trans. and ed. by Dr. A. A. Brill, copyright 1938 by Random House, Inc. Copyright © renewed 1965 by Gioia Bernheim and Edmund R. Brill. Reprinted by permission.

Contents

CONTENTS

Foreword

It is a terrible thing to come face-to-face with another human soul. It embarrasses us, strips us down in a way that no clothes can cover. The other who stands before us, equally uneasy and caught off guard, presents us with a silent but imperious challenge. How are we to engage with this intimate call for engagement amidst overwhelming sameness and disconcerting otherness?

The uncanny nakedness of this moment impels us to turn away in shame. But the instant we incline to do so an even more disturbing reality forces its way into our awareness. It is a moment just like this that we have been waiting for. Something deep in our being has been pining for such a meeting. The polite and superficial encounters that fill our days with arrangements, plans, and business as usual amount to nothing more than quotidian distractions in the face of what *soul* offers us. To turn away confronts us with the loss of a momentous opportunity. But an opportunity for what? We hardly know—even as it seems to us now, in our sidelong embarrassment, that we dare not pass it up.

Does the greater anxiety lie in entering more deeply into this undefended intimacy that threatens to abolish every shred of safety, or in scampering back to our illusory self-sufficiency, as flat and empty as it is? There are no rules for entering more deeply. We haven't the slightest idea how to seize this disturbing opportunity. Yet we quail before the prospect of letting it go. Impulse and hesitation bring us to an agitated halt, frozen like a mouse before the inscrutable stare of a snake. Or is that perhaps *our* blood, running cold beneath dry scales?

When soul meets soul, we fall into the hands of Eros, the wild-eyed god of union, confusion, transcendence, and sin. Eros is the lord of frightening promise. Every time he slips between us and our sister, mother, lover, child, or analysand, an awesome choice bifurcates before us. To engage or to betray? To risk dissolution and the death of everything we have known about ourselves on the strength of an unformed intimation of numinous encounter? Or to cling to safe and familiar routines at the risk of a lasting deadness at our core?

This dreadful golden moment when soul meets soul and the energies of Eros are conjured up, illumines every page of Robert Stein's classic—now finally available under its original and more accurate title, *The Betrayal of the Soul in Psychotherapy*. It unfolds before us as a document of soul. Not just a treatise on the *idea* of soul, although it is surely that but a phenomenology of soul, an explication of the living experience of soul. In stark contrast to all the sentimental new-agey books that flood the stores today with a fluffy, feel-good, and cuddly soul, Stein sticks to tough, unblinking realism. Only a man who has caught himself shamelessly in the act of turning tail, brought himself up short and turned back, could have written a book like this. Thus it is a document of Robert Stein's open-hearted and unflinchingly honest soul. Although—like every true document of soul—it is autobiographical to the bottom, *Betrayal* never loses its way in self-indulgence. Stein turns his work into a mirror where in his reflections we see our own soul: blushing, shamed, and full of promise.

Three themes are plaited into the braid of this book: (a) the struggle with incest whereby the soul is brought to life and given the scope to expand and flourish; (b) the betrayal of soul as a culturally *and psychotherapeutically* reinforced tragedy that affects us all; and (c) the need for a psychotherapy that engages with soul.

The awakening and development of soul. Soul is "a living pulse, a vital ever-changing energy within my body . . . unpredictable," and unavailable to objective verification (17). It forms the basis of my encounter with myself and with the self of another (18). Soul is a dimension of human experience—not a theological entity. It is an aspect of life and may conceivably go unnoticed. We must be awakened to soul lest we ricochet through the world untouched, isolated, and frantic.

Human life presents us with infinite opportunities to experience that erotic flow of energy that arises whenever soul meets soul. The parent-child dyad constitutes our first encounter. Soul energy moves through and extends far beyond the purely physical exchanges of feeding, rocking, and changing the infant. In the context of bodily satisfaction, energy circulates through mother and child, binding them, drawing them into a living togetherness where they find delight, fulfillment, and mutuality. Like a gradual awakening from dreamless sleep, the child comes to discover its living self reflected in the soul of its mother.

These earliest experiences have an oceanic, undifferentiated quality about them. Parent and child move into a numinous space of unity-amidst-difference, resting there in a gentle flow of eros that contains and satisfies. There is little that is personal in this encounter. Ten thousand years ago it was identical to what it is today, an archetypal experience, impersonal, and of overwhelming power. Neither parent nor child is capable of resisting this energy or giving it a different shape. But as the infant grows into a toddler, a young child, an adolescent, and an adult, *personality*—the unique otherness of the partners— gradually develops, and the archetypal ground-plan of the interaction becomes personalized. The meeting of soul with soul changes as the partners change, particularly as the child develops an ego. Through the course of these changes, we come to find out who we are as soulful beings far larger than our egos. We get in touch with that unpredictable and ever-changing energy that reveals our selves to us, as well as our capacity to meet other selves.

Even though our family members provide the first and most formative encounters with soul, and even though the bonds we form with them claim the highest honor of place in our lives, we cannot rest in the family forever. The incest prohibition sets our parents and siblings off limits for a full bodily experience of the soul-to-soul encounter. Robert Stein sees this as a critical road block, preventing an unconscious identification with the instincts. By halting the natural expression of our mating instinct, the incest taboo opens up new pathways for soul. We are left to imagine what we cannot carry out. Imaginal life begins in incest, the draw toward that which is forbidden to act upon but not to fantasize about.

Incest also forces us out of the family into encounters with individuals who have not lived a common life with us and not been known continuously from birth. Here, where the incest taboo does not hold sway, we are liable to the full depth of erotic confusion and anxiety. Falling in love, the experience which typically draws us away from our family of origin, brings us face to face with a soul more foreign than any we have known, and yet marked with an uncanny familiarity. That conviction that we were "meant" to meet or that we have known one another in a former life reveals the archetypal power of the encounter. The very beginning of our romantic involvement is as impersonal and undistinguished as that of the parent-infant dyad. We are Adam and Eve, Osiris and Isis, Tristan and Isolde; the same at the court of a first century Raja as in a modern urban tenement.

Again we are faced with the task of personalizing the archetypal ground-plan—getting to know ourselves and our partner, our soul and our partner's soul, against the background of oceanic intimations of oneness. Human life is satisfying and meaningful to the extent that we are engaged in a dialogue with soul. We are bowled over by the challenging appearance of soul in that naked, defenseless moment when we meet another in depth. But we cannot remain frozen in that fuzzy, glowing moment of terror and promise. The requirements of relationship and our own psychological growth require us to do the hard, exposing work of personalizing our encounter.

Romantic engagement draws the body, too, and the sexual instincts into play. If the incest taboo has done its work of opening the soul's imaginal capabilities, a link between sexuality and soul has already been established—albeit unconsciously. This makes it possible for sexuality to take its place in the interchange of soul with soul. Sexuality is freed from its masturbatory autonomy as merely a place where energy accumulates and demands release. It becomes a channel for personalizing the archetypal encounter. Intercourse—performed caringly and with attention to its mystery—concentrates and "tunes" the flow of erotic energy and plays an essential role in the dialogue between two souls. In the process, body and soul are integrated at a new level; ego and soul broaden the foundation of their on-going dialogue; and I encounter you more fully and transformatively. As a man, I become acquainted with my feminine receptivity (*anima*), and as a woman with my masculine power to penetrate the soul of my partner (*animus*).

The natural course of ensouled human life occurs as a series of erotically charged soul-to-soul encounters followed by personalizing, differentiating, and integrating the unconscious forces that soul calls into play. The soul-soul encounter is therefore the primary means for the growth and development of personality. Life is lived most intensely and deeply in these meetings. Truly *human* life is unthinkable without them. For all that, most of us rarely give soul a thought.

The betrayal of soul. Failure to engage with soul—i.e., its betrayal—is an all too frequent occurrence. As parents, we may be so impressed with the vulnerability of our baby and intimidated by our own responsibility that we never recognize the call of our child's soul. Some of us may see it well enough but be too frightened by the boundlessness of the oceanic feelings soul arouses. We may turn from our infant for our own protection. Or we may engage well enough as long as our infant is quite small and nothing more challenging is required than resting on the salty waves of soul. As soon as the personalizing process begins, however, we may turn tail. We may feel embarrassed, guilty, impotent, and foolish as the child develops an ego and wants to know who we are. Our unworthiness is revealed, and we want to hide behind our archetypal office as parent, and by this means to bring a to halt the personalizing process: "Shut up, I'm your father!"

If as parents we are afraid of our child's eagerly engaging soul, it is likely that our own soul was betrayed long ago by our parents. Undoubtedly, we have a poor relationship with our spouse's soul. There, too, the natural personalizing process may have been aborted early on. Perhaps we have even forgotten those heady days, early in our relationship, when Eros constellated the archetypes of anima and animus and engagement with our partner excited and frightened us with its awesome power. Probably we dissipated our anxiety in a head-long pursuit of orgasm—a procedure that suffices to produce children but neither to develop a mature relationship nor to prepare us to engage with the soul of our child.

All too many of us are wounded so badly that we dare not take on the soulful dimensions of life. Robert Stein sees this as a flaw rooted deep in our Western culture, which he calls the "incest wound." Primitive societies were relatively conscious of the incest problem. They lived in small communities in which nearly all members bore some blood relation to all the others. They had to organize themselves into cooperative factions (moieties) with rules and rituals for marriage and the raising of children. These symbolic structures enabled them to convert the powerful draw of incest into imaginal activities. They were conscious of their souls, lived in a world that was filled with soul, and knew something of engaging with soul. Their diseases were understood to be manifestations of soul-loss, and they developed rituals and tranced activities (especially shamanism) to restore the lost souls of their "wounded" fellows.

We, however, live in a world where soul has no place. The Renaissance kindled our interest in the material world, and experimental science has taught us the mind-boggling technological devices we can construct when we confine our attention to measurable facts. Philosophy since Descartes has emphasized our isolated subjectivity: we think, therefore we are. Over the past half millennium we have convinced ourselves that we are nothing but bodies moved by a rational ego. Soul has become for us either a quaint theological notion or a flaky, sentimental distraction. Together with our loss of soul, we have lost our appreciation for the imaginal, symbolic world where soul lives. For us, imagination has become merely a private, subjective, and frivolous distraction from the empirical world which alone is "real." We have become isolated rational egos because we have lost our appreciation of soul, the one dimension of human existence that connects us with one another. The terror we experience upon coming face-to-face with another human soul is no longer seen as a sublime mystery. For us it is the hallmark of neurotic anxiety. We dismiss it—or try to "cure" it—as though it were nothing but a fear of sex.

A quarter of a century ago, when Robert Stein wrote the first edition of this book and attributed our soul-impoverished life-style to our having forgotten the meaning of incest and its prohibition, we might have been able to read his thesis as merely the maundering of a physician and psychotherapist too deeply immersed in the writings of Freud and Jung. For who thinks of incest anymore? No matter that this is precisely his point. In the last ten or fifteen years, however, incest has become our obsession. Our daily papers and news broadcasts are filled with reports of child abuse and sexual harassment—some real, some imagined; and we have a devil of a time figuring out which is which.

Stein tells us that when our culture lost the rituals and symbolic understanding of incest and its taboo, all consciousness of the incest problem fell into the unconscious. We are no longer aware of incest but only of sexuality, which has taken on all the danger and sense of the forbidden that formerly belonged to incest. We are afraid of sex. We have become split off from our bodies which, alone, for us contain the sexual impulse. And we can no longer unite the masculine and feminine sides of our being. Because Eros continues to draw us to one another in the awful mystery of soul-to-soul engagement, we are afraid of Eros, too. We think that the erotic and the sexual are the same. We fear that every soul we meet is inviting us to a genital, masturbatory naughtiness which we may not be able to resist. We accuse one another of seduction, cock-teasing, and harassment because we can no longer recognize soul.

Mainstream psychotherapy is complicit in our cultural blindness. Its rituals were established nearly a century ago according to Freud's ideal of scientific detachment, the very same mentality that Western culture has been pursuing since the Renaissance. It pictures the encounter of therapist and patient on the model of two separate rational egos meeting to discuss dispassionately and to "analyze" the unconscious forces that interfere with the patient's attempt to live a rational life. The analyst is urged to be cool and emotionally uninvolved. In its most emphatic form, the ritual envisages an analyst who acts as a "blank screen" for the projections of the patient. The patient is to learn as little as possible about the personality of the analyst. Rather the patient's "projections" recreate the neurotic structure of his life in the form of a "transference neurosis" which can be dispassionately deconstructed.

There is no place in such a scheme for the naked and disturbing encounter of soul with soul. In fact, therapy amounts to a "strange distortion of the human connection," where one party strives for objective distance while the other is urged "to become completely involved and entangled emotionally" (134). Psychotherapy as usual is an inhumanly structured encounter that blatantly repeats the injurious frustrations of the child whose parent refuses to engage with his soul. While the therapist is seen as a scientist/technician who coolly observes and measures, the patient becomes merely an object to be inspected, probed, and readjusted.

In mainstream psychotherapy—as in our culture as a whole—the soulful human element is seen as a dangerous and destructive force that has to be held at bay. When Eros enters the space between therapist and patient, stirring up the terrible forces of soul meeting soul, we become convinced that something has gone wrong. We feel the overpowering draw to engage and the equally strong anxiety, shame, and confusion that Eros always generates. But we do not see it as an awe-inspiring mystery. It never dawns on us that this might be the first appearance of a healing and transformative energy. Rather we fall into a panic, terrified at the prospect of "sexually acting out."

FOREWORD

Psychotherapy as usual, in short, is as ignorant of the difference between Eros and sexuality as our culture at large. Soul is never considered. Emotional involvement is pathologized. The incest taboo is not appreciated as the means by which imagination is opened up. There is no appreciation of incest at all. The unconscious incest taboo manifests, instead, as a morbid fear of sexuality. Thus the psycho-therapeutic tradition of the last hundred years, while pretending to address the problem of the "incest wound," actually works to reinforce it. Traditional therapy amounts to a betrayal of soul.

Toward a psychotherapy of engagement with soul. If our most damaging wounds result from failed and aborted soul-to-soul encoun-ters, and if our deepest longing as human beings is to meet and be met by another soul, it is clear that an effective psychotherapy must develop rituals which enable this sort of engagement. Eros must be welcomed and appreciated as the transcendental agent who makes possible the healing of wounded souls. And if Eros is to become a third partner in our therapeutic meetings, therapists must become conscious of the full range of erotic feelings. As we have seen, Eros is a contradictory god. On the one hand he calls us to an undefended and naked engagement, full of emotion. If soul is to be engaged, the analyst must be prepared to enter this encounter as unreservedly as the patient. On the other hand, Eros inspires us with intimations of great danger—even the destruction of everything we have known about ourselves. Every erotic encounter with another soul conjures up the prospect of a disturbing transformation that makes us doubt that we are adequately prepared. These fears, too, must be taken seriously. Furthermore, the sexual impulse is not far behind. Indeed, the less we have explored our sexuality and integrated it, the more likely this imperious drive will move to the foreground of our awareness.

To engage erotically with another soul, therefore, we have to be able to hold the tension between the call for a naked and unrestrained encounter and the equally powerful alarm of impending destruction. "Eros is not only urging me toward union, it is also urging me toward restraint so that each involvement can unfold as a unique and original creation" (158). In the tension between these two forces of headlong union and cautious restraint, the incest taboo will be recovered and experienced consciously. To acquiesce with the arousal and yet to restrain our impulses to act upon it recreates the natural soulful human condition which primitive humanity knew very well but we have lost. It opens up the imaginal realm of soul, wherein fantasies about our partners and what they mean to us spill out in a stream of multivalent symbols.

When we flee from soul, we scurry back to the flat and sterile domain of mere rationality that is the problem. When, on the contrary, we plunge headlong into a literal, sexual union with our partner, soul is abandoned no less emphatically; for we have reduced ourselves to the merely bodily domain where the imaginal has no place. We have split off rational ego from instinctual body. Only in the tension between union and distance can soul be acknowledged and given the scope to open our eyes to new possibilities. This is the irrational and soulfully transforming reality that Jung has called the "transcendent function." Its only prerequisite—albeit a daunting one—is to hold the tension between opposites that cannot be reconciled rationally.

Apart from the abstract notion that an irrational solution will appear, Jung has given us few guidelines for what to expect when we hold the tension. Robert Stein, however, has suggested a very helpful blueprint for this process when it occurs between a pair of human beings undergoing a soul-to-soul encounter. Every such meeting occurs in an archetypal moment. We are parent and child, lover and beloved, guru and disciple, therapist and patient. The same always and everywhere. Every soul that engages with another soul begins the encounter as part of an impersonal dyad of mythic and oceanic proportions. When we cling to our office as parent, therapist, child, or patient, we block progress and arrest the movement of soul energy. The irrational solution, the reconciling of the opposites, begins with and takes the form of what Stein calls the "personalizing" process. It is a gradual course of becoming acquainted, of trying on and stripping away the impersonal mythic traits from ourselves and our partner. It elates us and makes us gods. It exposes wounds, inadequacies, and shame. It sets loose our imaginal capacities.

FOREWORD

A stream of fantasies reveals mythic dimensions in ourselves and in our partner. We project a great deal onto our partner. However unrealistic these projections may seem from a purely empirical standpoint, there's always a "hook" to hang them on. They always reveal something previously unknown about our analyst or our patient. This is the aspect of "trying on" and trying out the new mythic realities that Eros brings to a meeting of soul with soul. But there is a great deal of the impersonal and the inaccurate in these projections. The personalizing process requires us to share these emotional fantasies. To do so, the analyst may not retreat behind a "blank screen" but must participate in the process. Even when unexpressed, the analyst's fantasies will have an effect upon the relationship and upon the patient. They are a crucial aspect of the movement of soul energy and must be taken as seriously as are the emotional fantasies of the patient. In articulating them, the analyst does not cling to an archetypal identity as healer but allows his or her own personality to be revealed.

The process of sharing these imaginal realities opens them to critical reflection in which both parties, therapist and patient, refine the nature of their encounter. False illusions are stripped away. The defenses—the wished-for falsifications that make us feel safe and that stand in the way of transformation—are gradually shed. The personalization of an archetypal relationship is an empathic process of creative disillusionment. Yet as long as soul energy continues to flow between the partners, the archetypal ground-plan is not lost. Bodily impulses and sensations are appreciated anew in their imaginal potential. The merely literal recovers its symbolic and transformative dimension. As each partner phallically penetrates the other, each also opens up to and receives the other's penetration. In this way the masculine and feminine halves of each partner enter the process and begin to be integrated.

As long as the meeting between therapist and patient takes place within a "positive" rapport—a spirit of mutual trust and benevolent regard—the personalizing process may proceed without significant hitch. If so, the "incest wound" of the patient can be healed. For the patient is finally experiencing that his own soul is acceptable, valuable, and capable of engagement. But we may not always presume that this will be the case. Robert Stein's clear-sightedness does not permit him to overlook or to treat lightly the much more difficult situation in which a "negative" rapport dominates the interpersonal field. This is the so-called "negative transference," when the patient's woundedness cannot allow him to trust the process. In such a case, the analyst is seen as untrustworthy and damaging. Perhaps the analyst's "negative countertransference" is part of the problem.

Even in these most difficult cases, the personalizing of the archetypal ground-plan is essential. But here Stein cautions that the analyst may not assume that good intentions and hard work can accomplish the impossible. The most that can be hoped for is that the problem be identified and that both parties come to see that a dead-end has been reached: that two souls have encountered one another and discovered they cannot go on. They must learn *why* they cannot proceed and must part ways in the awareness that, although healing has not been effected, at least the wound has been recognized. A sorrowful termination without completing the work is not a total loss; for the patient's vague and oceanic sense of unworthiness has been specified, seen as the issue it is, and been raised to consciousness. Both parties may hope that another therapist may be found whose limitations will not prevent a trusting engagement with this particular form of woundedness.

It will be immediately apparent that *The Betrayal of the Soul in Psychotherapy* is very much a "politically incorrect" book. I can think of no higher praise for it. For to be "politically correct" is to acquiesce in all the simplicities and comforting banalities that society erects to give us a false sense of security and protect us from the harsh realities of life. The ideal of "political correctness" would seal us into the deceptive womb of what Jung calls "mass-mindedness." We think what everyone thinks and try to convince ourselves that we feel what everyone is expected to feel. To be "politically correct" is to shrink from our own unique individuality. It means to try to conform

FOREWORD

ourselves to a false sense of self, defined by the buzz words that assail us from all sides, demanding that we relinquish our profound misgivings. "Political correctness" divides the world into black and white and condemns us for trying to hold the tension between oversimplified alternatives. It denies that authentic living takes place mostly in the gray.

Robert Stein suffered a great deal for his outspoken honesty. He has been vilified for his dangerous but realistic view that an erotic encounter of soul with soul is the essential element in psychotherapy, and that to flee from this danger amounts to a betrayal of the very task that psychotherapy has set for itself. Implicitly, those who accuse him of advocating a "most dangerous method" have taken the position that avoiding mistakes is the first rule in psychotherapy. For Stein this is a hopelessly naive position. There will always be mistakes. No human relationship worthy of the name—including psychotherapy—can hope to proceed without both parties getting hurt, at least from time to time. The mistakes and the injuries are unavoidable. The only realistic way to proceed is to accept this fact in advance and to be prepared to recognize our mistakes when we make them and, thereby, to learn from them.

It is a terrible thing to come face-to-face with another human soul, and a daunting task to take on such encounters as one's life's work. Robert Stein did so in a spirit of humility. In this book he tells us some of the mistakes he has made and how he learned from them. His courage in writing the book was not heroic but humble. I observed him listening to his critics patiently. He never stood on a soapbox, and he never lost his awe in the face of soul. I thank him for that and am honored to be associated with a book that says so many of the things that need to be said because they are so frequently denied.

John Ryan Haule
November, 1997
Chestnut Hill, Massachusetts

xiii

Introduction to the Second Edition

In late August, 1983, Jungian analysts and trainees held a special Conference on Transference/Countertransference at Ghost Ranch in New Mexico. I had looked forward to hearing about the current work being done toward integrating contemporary psychoanalytic object-relations theory into Jungian theory and practice. The quality of the papers presented was outstanding, but I was amazed to see how this belated Jungian concern with working through the genetic aspects of the transference had activated all the fears of bad parenting. Listening to these papers in this magnificent, wide-open, free spirited Georgia O'Keeffe territory, I was shocked to see this regression to the medical model which still holds the analyst responsible for carrying consciousness and for maintaining structure and order. Fear of sexuality, of the instincts, of the unconscious, of the irrational, of the spontaneous movements of the soul prevailed. With very few exceptions, everyone seemed to agree with the view that the analyst's ego must protect the patient against the analyst's countertransference reactions and that therapeutic responsibility demands that the analyst always process the countertransference before exposing reactions. I was saddened to realize that a major theme of this book was not represented, namely, that, unless the analyst is free to be himself or herself, to reveal and to trust spontaneous instinctual reactions, the analysis will only perpetuate the soul-splitting ego psychology which prevails in our culture.

ROBERT STEIN

Contemporary psychoanalysis has moved its theoretical focus from the oedipal fantasy to the pre-oedipal fantasy: damaging developmental wounds occur in the process of the child's separation from its original symbiotic union with mother. The transference, so goes the fantasy, recreates this mother-child symbiotic merger, thus offering the possibility of a healing reconstruction of the personality. An important consequence of identifying the origins of the experience of oneness and wholeness with the literal mother-child symbiosis is that unifying experiences tend to be seen as regression. Viewing the transference/countertransference primarily from this perspective plunges the analyst into an identification with the all embracing, containing mother archetype and the patient into an identification with the innocent, needy, abandoned, helpless, dependent child archetype. Not only does this perpetuate a split in the Mother-Child archetype, but also the analyst becomes inflated by this identification with the all-powerful, all-nourishing, all-containing Great Mother. Often, at this Ghost Ranch Conference, some conscientious analyst would remind us that we must be very careful because our words carry such power for our patients. When an archetype speaks, words certainly do carry great power. But it is not *our* words, as analysts, that have such power but The Word. As soon as I realize that it is not my word, but The Word, and that The Word has as much power over me as over my patient, we can both join together as equals in relationship to this transpersonal power, this archetype. This move releases me from feeling that I must protect my patient by first processing, and predigesting my counter-transference reactions before I feed them back to this "fragile and helpless infant" whom I am trying to reconstruct into a healthy adult with a strong ego.

I have begun this introduction with these reactions to the Ghost Ranch Conference because this book is fundamentally: 1) an archetypal exploration of some of the fragmenting developmental wounds which cripple the soul's capacity for intimacy, union, wholeness, and creativity; 2) an attempt to develop a more soul-centered approach to the psychotherapeutic relationship and transference work. In contrast to the ego-centered psychoanalytic notion that the image of union has its origins in the symbiotic mother-child relationship, the archetypal perspective imagines the impulse toward union and wholeness as originating in *a priori* images such as the Sacred Marriage (*hierosgamos*) of the divine brother-sister pair, which Jung refers to as the incest archetype. Instead of viewing the soul's need to lose itself in merging with another as a regressive urge to unite with mother, I see the image of the mother-child symbiosis as one expression of the incest archetype. *This moves the soul's need for union, which is at the core of the transference phenomena, away from the parent-child archetype toward a transference model based on the equality and mutuality of the Brother-Sister pair.* The incest model frees the analyst from the illusion of being the carrier of consciousness and responsible for maintaining the protective, maternal therapeutic vessel. Since the Parent-Child archetype continues to inform the helping professions, as well as most of our cultural institutions, I see the development of the Brother-Sister model of psychotherapy as part of a larger evolutionary movement away from the power orientation of patriarchy and matriarchy toward eros-centered models of communal life which promote new levels of intimacy and equality between the sexes.

In alchemy, incest was exalted into a symbol of the supreme union of the opposites expressed as a combination of things which are related but of unlike nature.[1] While Jung recognized the importance of this symbol, he did not explore the relationship between the incest taboo and the developmental process through which this image is formed and integrated into the psyche. This book attempts to fill this gap. As long as the Freudian view of early childhood, ego development, and transference continues as the major influence in the modern psychotherapeutic endeavor, the ego-centered perspective will prevail. I believe an archetypal understanding of the deep incestuous developmental wounds to the psyche is essential for the further development of a soul-centered psychology and therapy.

A central theme of this book is the notion that the image of the sacred and eternal erotic union of the lover with the beloved, the

---

1. C. G. Jung, *Collected Works 14*, §664.

hierosgamos or incest archetype, is behind the experience of soul connection with another person, object, image, or idea. When this image is released, the physical body of the beloved is experienced as sacred. Such experiences of the embodied soul are always sensual and erotic. Since the sacred quality of life is a function of soul connection, when our erotic sensibilities are undeveloped, neglected, repressed, feared, the world tends to become de-souled.

To experience soul in a person or object is to feel a sensual connection to and appreciation of the beauty and sanctity of its living, erotic essence. Always, when souls touch, it is an erotic experience. Thus, when I feel a blockage of my sexual imagination, I cannot experience soul in the world. Without the free flow of erotic imagery, I am neither open to receive nor to enter into another soul. In Chapter One I describe how my own incest wounds contributed to a severe blockage of my sexual imagination. I keep emphasizing freeing *the imagination* because being uninhibited in the sexual act does not necessarily indicate that we are able to fully and consciously embrace our sexual images. Many people, for example, feel dead inside much of the time unless they are having a passionate sexual relationship. Feeling passionately in love temporarily removes the barriers and frees the images. But the old blockages return as soon as the passion begins to wane. Furthermore, as long as we are dependent on another person to release the flow of sexual imagery, we are not really free, and our connection to the soul in things is very tenuous.

If soul-connection is primarily dependent on the activation of the incest archetype, of images of the harmonious, sacred union of the masculine/feminine opposites, why is it so essential that we have a free and open channel to our sexual images? What difference does it make if I have difficulty consciously accepting images belonging to my polymorphous perverse, impersonal phallic, or sadomasochistic sexuality? What have such images to do with the image of the Sacred Marriage? Since we never know precisely what images will release the incest archetype, any type of imaginal blockage could interfere with our capacity for soul-connection. Secondly, the erotic nature of the *coniunctio* image tends to become spiritualized, to lose body (thus, soul), if there is any blockage of sexual imagery.

Because the erotic aspects of love attach and bind us to particular people and objects, overcoming the lusts of the flesh and moving to a higher, spiritual, universal love is often a basic tenet of religious life. Erotic love binds us to this world, while universal love or agape enables us to become free of our attachments to the material planes of existence. Well, this presents a problem. If erotic love is so essential to ensouling the world, how can we follow both the psychological and the spiritual paths, when each, in different ways, requires us to free ourselves of our physical attachments (projections), without de-souling them? In many ways the archetypal view of the incest mystery presented in this book addresses this issue.

Freud's view of incest revolves around the image of the child's literal desire for sexual union with the parent of the opposite sex. The archetypal view sees the image of the sacred union of the divine brother-sister pair, which is so essential to the experience of erotic love and soul-connection, as the key to the incest mystery. By moving the image of incest away from its literal attachments, a new path is created for understanding the process through which we become free of our literal bondage to particular people and objects, free from our projections, without losing soul.

Before ending this introduction, I want to include some reflections on the self-ego relationship which may facilitate reading this book. By locating the ego in the brain and describing it as a special organization of the mind, Freud perpetuated the Cartesian fallacy of "I think, therefore I am." To imagine that my sense of identity is located only in my brain, that my consciousness is a function only of my mind, is to make the rational mind the center and regulating instrument of the personality.

My senses of identity and being are not only functions of my mind. Mind consciousness is primarily a faculty for observing and sorting data. I feel no sense of my identity, my *I-ness*, when I am observing data, even if that data is about myself. No, my sense of identity occurs only when I experience my total being responding. What this means is that

xix

I am responding immediately and directly in my unique way to the full, unsorted mixture of the sensations, feelings, intuitions, thoughts, and images which I am experiencing and responding to the interaction.

The notion that the development of consciousness is dependent on the ego's ability to gain control over the unconscious and our anima-sensual nature is another manifestation of the Cartesianism which has shaped our modern concept of the ego. From this perspective, the lusts and passions of the body, the emotions, the instincts are a continual threat to the emerging ego. So mind/body, spirit/matter, conscious/unconscious are in eternal conflict with each other. While Jung accepted this Freudian description of ego development for the first half of life, he attempted to transcend it by postulating that the unconscious contained another principle (the Self) capable of reconciling this opposition. Jung describes the individuation process belonging to the second half of life as a recentering of the personality around the self. However, he emphasized that one must first develop an ego strong enough to withstand and confront the powerful regressive forces contained within the unconscious. Even in his last major work, Jung makes the following statement about the ego: consciousness consists in the relation of a psychic content to the ego. Anything not associated with the ego remains unconscious.[2]

The word *ego* refers to that part of the organism which perceives and experiences stimuli from within and without, to a conscious being who is aware of itself as a separate entity and is able to say *I*. Descartes identified the ego, the knowing subject, with the rational mind. Freud perpetuated this view of the ego, as well as the Cartesian attitude toward the body, emotions, and instincts. Therefore consciousness has become identified with a function of the rational mind and cerebral cortex. Jung rightly perceived the limitations and one-sidedness of this type of ego consciousness, leading him to postulate a superior consciousness which includes both conscious and unconscious. One wonders if he would have needed to seek for a superior consciousness

---

2. Jung, *CW 14*, §522n.

capable of uniting the opposites if he had not first accepted the Freudian-Cartesian ego. The identification of ego consciousness with the rational mind has in itself created much of the conflict between ego/unconscious, mind/body, and nature/nurture.

Ego is the Latin word for I. Freud used it as a direct translation of the German word *Ich.* Since the Freudian ego is certainly not identical to my sense of *I-ness,* I prefer to use the term self to describe this experience. In contrast to the ego, the self is primarily subjective and contained within every cell of the body. The self shapes everything which enters the soul, giving a unique perspective to all those universal experiences common to humankind, and it does not see the rational mind as necessarily in opposition to the unconscious but rather as a helpful ally in the soul's individuation. To identify the *I* with the mind and brain is a tragic error of modern psychology because it intensifies our loss of connection to soul and adds to our confusion about the source of individuality and consciousness. When we identify with the ego, not only do we lose contact with the true center of our individuality, but also the creative dialogue between self and ego, which is so essential to the soul's development, becomes confused and obstructed. *If I identify with my ego rather than with my self, I will always experience my soul as something other, something outside myself, while it is I who am really outside of my soul.* Only when I recognize that I and the self are one can I have a creative dialogue with my friend, ego, who can be detached and objective about both my inner experiences and my outer relationships.

With the ego's help, the self can step back periodically to view its creative work objectively. The ego might say, " that seems off to me, why don't you try moving it a bit," or it might say, "it seems to me you are making the same mistake that you made last time, why don't you try a new approach for a change," and so on. As with a friend, the self needs to consider what the ego says, but it is not necessarily the final word. Not at all. The self must inform the ego (as it would a friend) about what it feels, thinks, and experiences. In that way a dialogue is initiated which is essential to the process of shaping the soul. But when ego and self are in conflict, only the self can effect a reconciliation of the opposites. When we engage in such a dialogue and identify with the ego, more often than not the rational mind becomes alienated from the self because it feels responsible for the final decision. The ego is capable of sorting out information only in a rational, orderly fashion and making an either/or choice at best. The type of intuitive, enlightening leap which alone can unite opposites must come through the self. The self shapes everything which enters the soul, including the ego.

For me, the self is not a superhuman Christ-like or Buddha-like being, resting in a state of wholeness and cosmic harmony. This Eastern view of The Self obliterates the uniqueness of each self and makes the ego the carrier of individuality. While I like the image of each self originating from a divine scintilla, this does not make the self and the Creator one. The deified image of The Self has little to do with that which makes us unique. The mistaken notion of the self as something far away and difficult to obtain prevents us from recognizing that the self is right here, right now in each individual's unique way of seeing and experiencing and in our bodily centers of consciousness as well as in our mental consciousness. Neither, in my opinion, is the self the archetype of order, the union of all opposites as symbolized by the circle, square, quaternity, mandala, hermaphrodite, *coniunctio,* etc., as Jung describes it. These images of wholeness and completion are archetypes and, as such, are not unique. I prefer to imagine the self as my unique way of experiencing, expressing, and relating to the archetypes, and to the Gods, as they enter my soul. The whole range of human experience from the highest to the lowest belongs to the self. One can experience disharmony, turmoil, emptiness, neediness, greediness, lust, jealousy, envy, hate, etc., as well as union and wholeness, and still be very much in and with the self. No, the self is not some difficult, unattainable goal which only saints and heroes achieve but the most basic thing in life, our essence and reason for being.

We have become split because we have come to mistrust and fear the self, and psychology has only intensified this catastrophe by devoting most of its efforts toward strengthening the Cartesian-Freudian ego. The quest for wholeness and completion is fundamental to the human condition and essential for psychological development. While this impulse may arise from the self, wholeness is not really a quality that describes the nature of the self. Depth psychology is still in a muddle about the concepts of self and ego. Further clarification and development are needed or, as we have seen, Jung's great contributions toward an archetypal and soul centered psychology may soon end in supporting yet another school of ego psychology.

Robert Stein
September 1983

Introduction

This book originated out of failure: the failure of my own analysis—in spite of its enormous benefits in expanding consciousness—to heal the original wounding split within my own nature, and my consequent failure as a therapist to help others who had similar psychic injuries. After considerable soul searching and an attempt to seek further analytical help for myself, it became clear to me that there was something in the very nature and structure of the psychotherapeutic situation that tended to reinforce the separation. I was forced to reevaluate the goals and limits of psychotherapy, to see if it was possible to change the ritual so that a healing resolution of the mind/body and love/sex dichotomy could occur. The purpose of this book is to share the results of my efforts. My conclusions are both old and new.

Freud was the first to recognize the incestuous origins of humanity's split between love and sex, between sensual feelings and feelings of tender affection. The discoveries he made in exploring the vicissitudes of the Oedipus complex are the foundation of psychoanalysis. He clearly demonstrated some of the psychological effects of the incestuous triangle, the Oedipus complex, and his finding have withstood the test of time. However, his conclusions about the nature and function of the incest taboo in human development are questionable and in need of reevaluation.

According to Freud's theory of the Oedipus complex, the male child's sexual desire for his mother gradually reaches an intensity whereby he wants to get rid of his father so that he can have his mother for himself. At the same time he loves and admires his father so that he is thrown into a love/hate ambivalence. But the boy finally represses his sensual desires for his mother, as well as his hate for his father, because of his fear of castration. He does this through a process of identification with and introjection of the father or parents into the ego. This interjected parental authority establishes the kernel of the superego, which acts as a severe internal force that perpetuates the prohibition against incest. Ultimately the superego also becomes the carrier of other societal values. Thus the resolution of the Oedipus complex is largely dependent on a strong superego which is able to successfully repress the incest desire. As Freud puts it, "the process described is more than a repression; when carried out in the ideal way it is equivalent to a destruction and abrogation of the complex."[1] A corresponding development occurs in the female, but Freud never felt on firm ground with regard to how the process was effected in a girl.

Freud believed that not only was individual development dependent on such a process, but he hypothesized that a similar process was responsible for the beginnings of culture. Borrowing from Darwin, he proposed a hypothetical primal horde at a remote period of time, dominated by a violent, jealous father, who kept all the females for himself and drove away the growing sons. Pursuing this fantasy Freud imagined that:

> One day the expelled brothers joined forces, slew and ate the father, and thus put an end to the father horde. Together they dared and accomplished what would have remained for them singly impossible . . . Of course these cannibalistic savages ate their victim. This violent primal father had surely been the envied and feared model for each of the brothers. Now they accomplished their identification with him by devouring him and each acquired a part of his strength. The totem feast, which is perhaps mankind's first celebration, would be the repetition and commemoration of this memorable, criminal act with which so many things began, social organization, moral restrictions and religion.

1. Sigmund Freud, "The Passing of the Oedipus-Complex," *Collected Papers, Vol. 2*, London: Hogarth Press, 1953, 269.

INTRODUCTION

> The brothers . . . hated the father who stood so powerfully in the way of their sexual demands and their desire for power, but they also loved and admired him. After they had satisfied their hate by his removal and had carried out their wish for identification with him, the suppressed tender impulses had to assert themselves. This took place in the form of remorse; a sense of guilt was formed which coincided here with the remorse generally felt . . . What the father's presence had formerly prevented they themselves now prohibited . . . They undid their deed by declaring that the killing of the father substitute, the totem, was not allowed and removed the fruits of their deed by denying themselves the liberated women. Thus they created two fundamental taboos of totemism out of the sense of guilt of the son, and for this very reason these had to correspond with the two repressed wishes of the Oedipus complex . . .[2]

With this fantasy Freud was able to achieve two things. Firstly, he gave a historical explanation for the origins of the incest taboo and culture, and secondly, he established a phylogenetic hypothesis which corresponded to his theory of individual development based on the Oedipus complex. From these descriptions, it is clear that Freud believed that the origins of culture and individual human development are both dependent on the *repression* of incestuous sexual drives. In his view the incest taboo was created only to serve this purpose.

The main theme of this book revolves around what I believe to be a more meaningful and accurate understanding of the incest mystery. These differences will be more easily understood if we first examine some of the basic assumptions upon which Freud developed his incest theories.

Freud's theories are deeply rooted in the metaphysics of scientific materialism, which reduces all aspects of the human organism to physical-chemical processes. In a superb investigation of the philosophical premises underlying Freud's concepts, Yankelovich and Barrett state that Freud's concept of the "mental apparatus" is "nothing

---

2. Sigmund Freud, "Totem and Taboo," *The Basic Writings of Sigmund Freud*, New York: Modern Library, 1938, 915-17.

less than a psychological surrogate for the Newtonian postulates of inertia and conservation of energy. Its function is only regulatory (though just how it regulates is left unspecified) and regulatory only to secure a steady and constant state."[3]

Thus in Freud's view instincts function entirely to relieve the somatic tensions of the organism. "The instincts are all qualitatively alike and owe the effect they produce only to the quantities of excitation accompanying them, or perhaps further to certain functions of this quantity."[4] These teeming, undifferentiated, blind instinctual energies function only to protect the somatic equilibrium of the organism. There is nothing in Freud's concept of the mental apparatus to indicate that human instincts function in a uniquely human way to shape the psyche. Quite the contrary–external influences alone, through the formation of ego and superego, are responsible for human psychological development. Freud equated ego with reason, culture and sanity, and instincts with uncontrolled passions and animality.

Structurally, Freud conceived the psyche as an apparatus composed of three portions: id, ego, and superego. The id "contains everything that is inherited, that is present at birth, that is fixed in the constitution— above all, therefore, the instincts which originate in the somatic organization . . ."

"Under the influence of the real, external world which surrounds us, one portion of the id has undergone a special development . . . which henceforward acts as an intermediary between the id and the external world. This region of our mental life has been given the name ego."[5]

"The ego represents what we call reason and sanity, in contrast to the id which contains the passions."[6]

---

3. Daniel Yankelovich & William Barrett, *Ego and Instinct*, New York: Random House, 1970, 48.

4. Sigmund Freud, "Instincts and Their vicissitudes," *Collected Papers, Vol. 4*, London: Hogarth Press, 1953, 66.

5. Sigmund Freud, *An Outline of Psychoanalysis*, London: Hogarth Press, 1955, 2.

6. Sigmund Freud, *The Ego and the Id*, London: Hogarth Press, 1947, 30.

INTRODUCTION

The superego forms within the ego as a consequence of prolonged parental influences. It includes "not merely the personalities of the parents themselves, but also the racial, national and family traditions handed on through them as well as the demands of the immediate social *milieu* which they represent."[7] The superego, then, is comprehended as an internal parental image which upholds societal values and acts as the voice of conscience.

Let us consider one last essential premise of Freud's theories: his explanation of the process through which the ego introjects. As I understand this theory, the undifferentiated sexual energies (ego and its exponent, the libido) are first stored up in the ego. This state is called primary narcissism and it continues until the ego begins to attach some of the libido to objects—to change narcissistic libido into object libido. A characteristic of libido is mobility so that it tends to remain only temporarily attached to objects, except where fixations occur. Thus the libido is withdrawn, like the "pseudopodia of a body of protoplasm," and the external object is introjected into the ego.[8]

As we can see from this formulation, the psyche is formed entirely by the introjection of those external objects we encounter during our life span. We do not inherit images or knowledge from our ancestors. How is it that we inherit so many physiological and anatomical characteristics, but that our psyche contains no uniquely human qualities at birth? Surely such a formulation is another manifestation of the severe mind/body split which continues to afflict Western humanity. While Freud frequently refers to the idea of the inheritance of memory traces from our human ancestors—i.e., the memory of the original deed of killing the father—in his psychodynamic theories the psyche seems to end up as a *tabula rasa* in the newborn infant.

Why would anyone want to begin with the premise that the instincts in a newborn infant are basically the same as in animals?

---

7. Freud, *An Outline of Psychoanalysis*, 4.
8. *Ibid.*, 8.

Well, if one believes that a person's ego consciousness, with its unique capacity for reasoning, is the only quality which differentiates people from animals, then it might make sense. After all, the newborn infant does not seem to possess any more rationality or consciousness than other animals. Couple this with the Cartesian bias which views the body as a machine governed only by mechanical laws, then the logic of Freud's choice becomes clear; if only the ego has soul (or psyche), and there is no visible evidence of an ego in the newborn infant, then we have no basis to assume that this organism is governed by processes other than the same physical-chemical processes which govern all other organisms.

If we abandon the Cartesian dualism and scientific materialism which underlie Freud's theories of instincts and psychic development, we are then free to hypothesize that we inherit not only a physical-chemical structure from our ancestors, but a psyche as well. What is psyche? It is the Greek word for soul, life, breath. So we must consider the concept of soul if we want to know what psyche is.

From time immemorial the soul has been viewed as an immortal animating life force which enters the body and assumes its form at the moment of conception or during pregnancy, leaving the body again at death. So far, the id in Freud's concept, except for the idea of immortality, might correspond to this life force. But the soul is more than this. It is also the carrier of humanity's psychic history and the source of a directing intelligence which, in the ancient view, was primarily responsible for the shaping of the individual's life and destiny—a far cry from the blind instinctual energies of Freud's id.

If such intelligent principles do indeed exist, then they must belong to humanity's instinctual heritage. But we shall never be able to explain how these instincts work if we remain bound to Freud's concept that instincts function only to relieve the somatic tensions of the organism.

If an instinct contains a directing intelligence, it must be capable of expressing itself in mental forms as well as in physical reactions. As we have seen, Freud's concept image formation is due to the introjection of objects from the external world. Now even among animals, modern investigators have demonstrated that an internal image must be released before an instinctual reaction occurs. For example, the bill of the herring gull is yellow, with a red spot at the end of the lower mandible. Using cardboard dummies in natural colors, Tinbergen[9] found that the red spot was the essential stimulus for releasing the feeding instinct in the baby gull. The gull had little or no response to a dummy lacking the red patch.

Such findings indicate that an instinctual response is dependent on the release of internal images innate to the perceptual system of the organism. These findings indicate also that the instinctual response is far more complex than a simple biological reflex. Jung's concept of the archetype as an inherited, preexisting psychic disposition is supported by such experiments.

For Jung the archetype is a formative principle of instinctual power, which can express itself in bodily reactions or through mental representations (images and ideas).[10] The archetype is the depository of all human experiences right from its earliest beginnings.

> Not, indeed, a dead deposit, a sort of abandoned rubbish-heap, but a living system of reactions and aptitudes that determine the individual's life in invisible ways—all the more effective because invisible . . . it is also the source of the instincts, for the archetypes are simply the forms which the instincts assume. From the living fountain of instinct flows everything that is creative; hence the unconscious is *not merely conditioned by history, but is the very source of the creative impulse.*[11]

Now that the concept of archetype has been introduced, the

---

9. N. Tinbergen, *The Study of Instinct*, London: Oxford UP, 1951, 29-31.
10. C. G. Jung, "On the Nature of the Psyche," *CW 8*, New York: Pantheon Books, 1960, §416-17.
11. C. G. Jung, "The Structure of the Psyche," *CW 8*, New York: Pantheon, 1960, §339. (Italics added).

contrast between Freud's view and my view of the incest mystery can be clearly defined. I begin with several assumptions concerning the nature and function of instincts. One such assumption is that humanity's unique course of development, including ethical values and social organization, is an instinctively based disposition. Another is that instincts originate from inherited transcendent principles—the archetypes—located in the psyche (or soul). Because the soul continually circulates throughout every cell of the body, we cannot speak of a specific somatic location for the psyche (in this case the brain) or for the archetypes. Thus the capacity for intelligence and consciousness is contained in every cell and not limited to the brain and rational mind. The archetype is viewed as an inherent disposition which is capable of releasing uniquely human instinctual patterns of imagery, thought, feelings, and behavior.

Based upon the above premises, we can assume that in spite of the instinctual similarities between a newborn infant and animals, human instincts are different. We have little difficulty accepting the instinctual origins of such unique and fantastic behavior as dam building in beavers or migration in birds, but Western people continue to resist the idea that their own unique behavior is in any way instinctual. Of course this metaphysical bias has a long history which can be summed up by St. Thomas Aquinas' view that "the behavior of man depends on reason, whereas all animals are governed by instinct." We always return to this same theme which prevails throughout Freud's theories, that it is the ego and the capacity to reason which alone differentiates him from animals.

My premise is that not only is our ability to reason unique, but so is our sexuality, our capacities for love and relatedness, our imagination, our language and so on, and I *do not accept the idea that our capacity to reason is responsible for all these differences.* On the contrary, I shall attempt to show that the main function of the incest taboo is to stimulate the growth of our uniquely rich imagination which goes hand in hand with our unique capacities for love, service and, dedication.

An archetypal view of instincts presupposes that when the

suckling instinct is released in an infant, for example, the infant begins sucking on the mother's nipple because of internal images as well as physiological mechanisms which compels the baby to do so. In the same way, a child relates to maternal attention in a typically human manner because of the release of an internal archetypal image of the mother-child connection. And so it goes in relationship to father, siblings and others. In other words all the typical forms of human relatedness which we have ever known— including sexual union—have become part of our archetypal inheritance. Even the idea that one must learn how to have sexual intercourse is simply another manifestation of how much our modern ego is cut off from its instinctual roots. Surely, animals must be directed by an internal image of sexual union, for they have little difficulty with the act even though they may never have witnessed it before. A virginal bitch in heat, for example, when there is no male around, will often mount other bitches not in heat and perform the rhythmical sexual movements typical of the male. One cannot help feeling that the bitch is acting out of an internal image which includes the male half of the union. This idea is not surprising if we take a moment to examine our sexual fantasies. If we should have sexual fantasies, our images will often involve both the male and female partners. Duality and polarity seem to be inherent characteristics of the archetype.

Within the family situation there exists the potential for the following archetypal constellations: Mother-Father; Mother-Son; Mother-Daughter; Father-Son; Father-Daughter; Brother-Sister; Brother-Brother; Sister-Sister. What this means is that a child is capable of experiencing all of these archetypal combinations regardless of his or her sex. While these archetypes refer to internal images, they are initially released by and experienced in relationship to an external object (mother, father, sibling). Once released, however, all the images belonging to humanity's history of this typically human experience begin to enter the child's psyche. These ideas are central to an understanding of my views about the meaning and mystery of incest.

Anthropological studies have shown that in primitive societies the strict regulations surrounding incest are designed primarily to prevent sexual relations between brother and sister not between parent and child. Most tribesmen find the idea of sleeping with their mothers ridiculous, but they are highly touchy about any suggestion of a sexual relationship with their sisters. Freud's view that the main purpose of the incest taboo is to prevent sex between parent and child is not substantiated by anthropological evidence.

Many anthropologists believe that the strong protective instincts which parents feel toward their young, plus the age disparity, should probably be sufficient to prevent sexual relations. What, then, is the purpose of having such a taboo between parent and child if it is not to inhibit sexuality between them? I shall attempt to show that, in relationship to the parents, the incest taboo functions primarily to make the union between mother and father sacred, thereby stimulating the formation of such archetypal images as the sacred union of the divine couple, the *hierosgamos*. Such images are essential for psychological growth and wholeness. In the brother-sister relationship, the taboo does indeed function to prevent concrete sexual involvement. Psychologically, however, it serves to stimulate the child's imagination to begin the uniquely human fascination with erotic and romantic imagery.

Freud's mechanistic philosophy could only lead to a concrete view of sexuality and incest. He could not entertain the idea that the incest taboo itself might be part of instinctual human sexuality. Nor could he conceive of the sexual instinct inhibiting itself in order to stimulate and pursue internal images rather than to achieve somatic gratification. I am, in contrast to this view, suggesting that the sexual instinct is far from a blind, undifferentiated drive, that it contains an intelligent will and the capacity to transform itself.

. The heart of the matter is that Freud viewed the sexual instinct— as he did all instincts—as a blind drive seeking only to relieve somatic tensions. Because he felt that no instinct could possibly be responsible for human development and culture, so the incest taboo could never be instinctive. I am in complete agreement with Freud's belief that the incest taboo is responsible for humanity's unique development. But as to the how of it we are at opposing poles.

For Freud, "it is not possible for the claims of the sexual instinct to be reconciled with the demands of culture."[12] And he reasons that this "irreconcilable antagonism . . . has made man capable of ever greater achievements, though, it is true, under the continual menace of danger, such as that of the neurosis to which, at the present time, the weaker are succumbing."[13] I would think so. Such conclusions are largely based on Freud's view that the sexual instinct can be satisfied only by concrete fulfillment. Therefore when the sexual instinct is obstructed in its desire for the parent or sibling, naturally it will be eternally antagonistic to the ego as it attempts to uphold cultural values. And from this point of view, for the sexual instinct, sublimation can at best be only a poor substitute.

In my opinion not only has Freud failed to grasp the true psychological significance of the incest mystery, but in settling for the irreconcilable antagonism between the rational and animal-sensual portions of the soul, he has succeeded in perpetuating the fragmenting effects of Cartesian dualism in his system of psychotherapy. He ends up glorifying the rational mind as the supreme regulating authority and ends with a distrust for all the spontaneous natural responses of humanity's animal instinctual nature. Such an attitude is anti-life and destructive to the human connection.

Freud's whole system of therapy, including the role and function of the therapist, is based on this distrust of instinctual nature. Not only is psychoanalysis dominated by this fear of the instincts but so are most other forms of psychotherapy. As far as I know, all existing schools of psychotherapy hold that one of the main functions of the therapist is to shed light, to bring consciousness. But consciousness is understood to mean ego consciousness, which means that the therapist must always attempt to maintain a certain distance and objectivity. I *believe this ego distancing of psychotherapists is a distinct*

---

12. Sigmund Freud, "The Most Prevalent Form of Degradation in Erotic Life," *Collected Papers, Vol. 4*, London: Hogarth Press, 1953, 216.

13. *Ibid.*, 216.

consequence of this distrust of *the instincts.* Further, I believe that it is not only unnecessary, but that it tends to perpetuate, rather than heal, the fragmenting effects of the Oedipus complex.[14] Throughout the book we shall return to this issue, but even now one can begin to see the enormous implications of this view of incest which I am attempting to present.

The theoretical formulations of modern psychology continue to be dominated by Cartesian metaphysics. Consequently the concept of the ego has, for all practical purposes, become synonymous with the rational mind. "*Cogito, ergo sum:* I think, therefore I am." This assumption that humanity exists as a unique entity only because of our capacity for rational thought is still the metaphysical base which prevails in our culture. For Descartes, the body, with its animal-sensual nature, is viewed as a substance distinct from the mind and subject only to mechanical laws. The body is passive while the mind is active and capable of free will. Because the rational mind can control and overcome the animal passions, it is superior to the emotional-body roots of human nature. *The mind is moved by soul while the body is moved only by animal spirits. Only the mind has soul.* The prime mover is God whose directing intelligence is continually manifesting itself in the rational mind. God has implanted motion in the human body and all other matter, but then He has abandoned all matter. Mechanical laws govern the material world. Humanity obeys the same laws since an individual is nothing but a more complex form of organization of the same processes that dominate other aspects of nature.[15]

In one sense this book is an attempt to break free of the Cartesian system, which not only denies the importance of the unification of mind and body but also works on the principle that people must

---

14. Henceforth the term "incest wound" will be used rather than Oedipus complex. I believe it is more descriptive of the damaging developmental effects of the incestuous triangle; further, Freud only views the Oedipus complex as damaging if it persists beyond the onset of the latency period.

15. Frank Thilly, *A History of Philosophy*, New York: Henry Holt, 1927, 272 f.

overcome the confusion which body brings to mind. My approach to human psychology reflects a radically different attitude toward Nature than the Cartesian model, which assumes that the rational mind alone has the knowledge and power to determine what a person must do with Nature. My assumption (an ancient one) is that Nature, including human nature, contains within itself a directing intelligence (soul) which is the source of all knowledge concerning the nature of a person's being and becoming. The rational mind needs to allow itself to be instructed by Nature, to use its imaginative activity to give the best possible expression to the instinctual-emotional-bodily roots of human desire. When the rational mind is cut off from its connection to the body and is functioning autonomously, basic human needs are abused and distorted. So long as twentieth century humanity continues to approach this dilemma with the assumptions of Cartesian metaphysics, there is no hope of reestablishing a new, harmonious and meaningful connection with basic human needs. Nature will continue to be viewed as an interesting machine, as an object for scientific investigation which can be controlled once we understand more about the causal relationship between its various moving parts.

Let me briefly give some idea of my method of investigating the psyche. Primarily I give supreme value to the sensations and emotions which I experience within my body. I assume that my subjective bodily experience generally contains some universal truth, and I have tried in this text to extract the universal from the personal. For example, if I acknowledge jealousy in a particular situation, I may attempt to search for some element in this experience which goes beyond my own personal needs to the root of some general human need. Clearly this approach is in opposition to the Cartesian view that universal truth can arise only from pure thought and that emotional-bodily experiences can only hinder one's quest for truth.

No healing of the conflict between the spirit and the flesh is possible so long as one's animal-instinctual nature is considered inferior to mind and psyche, which is an attitude common to both Freud and Jung. *Consequently both of their systems tend to*

perpetuate the soul splitting effects of the mind/body dichotomy.
This book begins with a discussion of this problem. Chapter Two
is primarily a critique and reevaluation of Freud's theory of
instincts and Jung's archetypal theory. Both of these theories are
clearly influenced by the same prejudicial attitude toward the basic
instincts—the superiority of mental functions over emotional
bodily functions. A critique of Freud's death instinct theory will
come later in part Four.

As the title of this book suggests, the main theme is the incest taboo
and its significance for the development of human love. It is surprising
how many studies of human cultural development have been made without
any attempt to examine the significance of the universal existence of the
incest taboo. No other structural characteristic of the human community
has remained so fundamentally unchanged throughout history, from the
most primitive to the most sophisticated modern culture. No known
culture, past or present, permits sexual relations between mother and
son, father and daughter, brother and sister.[16] The universal existence
of this taboo, and the fact that there is no evidence of its existence
among animals, would suggest that it may be a key factor in the
humanization process.

Part Two of this book considers the psychological and cultural
significance of incest. The view is developed that the origins of the
Occident's disturbed relationship to instinctual roots can be traced to
the loss of connection to the meaning and mystery of incest.

In Part Three specific aspects of masculine and feminine
psychology are discussed. There is an attempt to demonstrate that for
modern men and women the obstructions to psychological
development are largely a consequence of false assumptions and a
damaged relationship to the sexual instinct.

Still alive or buried in the human psyche are such phallic Gods
of ancient Greece as Pan, Priapus, Dionysus, and such female
Goddesses as Demeter, Persephone, and Aphrodite. While these forces

---

16. The exceptions are always a ritual re-enactment of the union between
God and Goddess, as in the Egyptian dynasties, for example, or in orgiastic rites.

are present (as are all archetypes) in both sexes, there is no doubt that women tend to identify more with these Goddesses symbolizing mother, maiden, and erotic love. Since an archetypal instinct theory holds that cultural forms, even though they may have become calcified or monstrous, reflect an inherent human disposition, we need not engage in the nature/nurture controversy surrounding the issue of feminine psychology.

Of course women are right to resist being shoved into these oppressive archetypal boxes. On the other hand, we all desperately need the renewal and fertility which the Goddesses bring. God is not dead, but surely the great ancient Goddesses have fallen into an abyss. What we have instead is saccharine, phallic rejecting imitations of the Great Mother, and plastic, sexless, playboy models of the "golden" Goddess. Many women use their aphrodisiac powers to manipulate men, but few are able, nowadays, to surrender to the Goddess and allow her great renewing love to enter the world. I do not blame them. If the erotic sense is not in a harmonious connection to the maternal, Aphrodite is nothing but a "wanton hussy," not to be trusted in any relationship. Out of her all-powerful yearning to melt into oneness with the beloved, all worldly considerations are forgotten, no honorable bond is sacred to her, and she is not averse to savagely destroying anyone who attempts to resist her.

A frequent consequence of the incest wound is a disturbed relationship to the maternal instinct, the receptive feminine principle in the human psyche. True openness, acceptance, and care for oneself or for others is not possible so long as the mother archetype remains closed and rejecting. The redemption of love and sexuality can, therefore, follow only in the wake of the gradual transformation of the inner mother.

In Part Four we explore the nature of Eros, and its function in psychological development. An attempt is made to substantiate the hypothesis that Eros rather than reason is the crucial humanizing factor in the human psyche. Following the ideas of Plato and Jung, Eros is understood to be that quality in the human soul which is responsible for human relatedness and psychic connection. While it includes the erotic, it is not identical to the demonic passion evoked by the Greek god of that name. A detailed discussion of the nature of Eros forms the main body of this section.

Part Five contains a detailed discussion of my views concerning the nature, use, and misuse of the transference phenomenon in psychotherapy. An archetypal view of transference leads to quite a different understanding of this phenomenon than does the psychoanalytic view. In fact in the final chapter of this book, some fundamental questions are raised concerning the advisability of using the transference phenomenon as a therapeutic instrument. This final chapter also presents my conclusions about how analysis can become a more satisfactory and complete psychotherapeutic ritual.

PART ONE

The Betrayal of the Animal

CHAPTER ONE

Psychotherapy: Freud and Jung

Psychotherapy is still a long way from achieving even the limited goal of healing an individual's damaged relationship to one's instincts. So long as a patient's instincts are at war with mind and spirit, psychological healing and the unification of the personality is obstructed. Both Freud and Jung agree that the integration of the instinctual-emotional life is a central aim of therapy. Nevertheless their analytical systems tend to perpetuate a continued abuse of our animal instincts rather than a creative resolution of the conflict.

When I started my practice as a Jungian analyst, I considered myself superior to my Freudian colleagues because I felt able to be open and natural with my patients while they were required to protect themselves behind the doctor's persona of scientific detachment. Not until I was suddenly hit by a severe anxiety attack and a painful bodily symptom did I begin to realize that I had deluded myself about my openness.

One of my patients, a disturbed woman, had been carrying on for weeks about the sexual aggressiveness of men as opposed to her own purity, innocence, and lovingness. One day she related how she had innocently accepted a ride with a man who then tried to force her to have intercourse. With obvious relish she went into every detail of what the man had said and done to her. I was knowledgeable enough, even then, to realize the seductive elements in her need to give such elaborate details. But I had no idea how all this was affecting me until I was overwhelmed with fearful anxiety and dizziness followed by severe pain in my penis. The attack soon passed, but I was left absolutely drained and feeling that I had been stabbed by a treacherous assailant.

After this painful and shocking experience, I immediately tried to examine my relationship to this woman and analyze what it had triggered off in me. It was not easy because whatever the element was, it was obviously something I had not uncovered after all my years in personal and training analysis. Everything seemed to point to an unresolved sexual problem on my part, but it was some time before the nature of my difficulty began to unravel itself. This book is a direct consequence of my attempt to understand and heal the wound that was opened up by this experience.

Unfortunately the symptom which I have described continued to recur whenever I had to listen to certain kinds of sexual material. In fact, it continued for about two years and it was so disturbing–I cannot describe the horror and despair I experienced–that I thought I would have to leave my profession; whoever heard of an analyst who could not listen to sexual material? Let me explain to you the essence of what I finally realized about myself.

It soon became clear that my attacks were caused by my fear of opening up to the experience of my own aggressive, lustful sexual fantasies, which my patient's pornographic stories had provoked. But why did I have such fear? I had spent years exploring the full range of my infantile, heterosexual, homosexual, and orgiastic sexual fantasies, and I had no conscious fear any longer. Was it the situation perhaps? Was I fearful that if I opened up to my fantasies I might become overwhelmed and attack my patient? Yes, this did indeed turn out to be a big part of my fear. Rationally, I knew there was little chance of this happening even if I were aroused, but it was a long time before I could risk this possibility in the analytical situation.

Finally, I was able to trace my fear to its incestuous origins. The sexual taboo in the analytical situation, plus the archetypal parent-child relationship which it constellates, activates both the horror of and fascination for incest whenever sexual feelings are experienced. In addition to this, the hypocritical innocence of my patient triggered in me the release of an enormous amount of repressed anger toward several of my older sisters, who, in my early adolescent years, had excessively provoked me sexually and then had denied it. To show how deep all this goes, last night, while I was working on this book, I had a dream in which I was trying to get one of my sisters to face up to what she had done to me when we were young, and she still claimed she had no memory that anything sexual had happened between us.

In psychoanalysis the patient is encouraged to experience emotionally and verbally to express all sexual fantasies. But what happens to the analyst, who is supposed to remain detached and objective? One thing is sure, whenever the incest mystery is touched upon, sexuality becomes charged, and it is impossible to remain uninvolved unless one is able to detach oneself from the experience—which is precisely what the analyst must do if he is to maintain his objective stance. But if it is the archetypal relationship between analyst and analysand which activates the incestuous sexuality, it cannot be a one-sided thing.

As long as the analyst is not also free to experience and verbally express his own sexual fantasies, the chances are that the analysand will be burdened with carrying the whole bag–the analyst's unconscious fantasies as well as his or her own. It is impossible, in my experience, to know what belongs to whom unless the analyst and analysand are mutually open about their sexual fantasies. Lacking this possibility two things tend to happen: 1) if the analysand does reveal sexual fantasies, they tend to be fragmented and cut off from emotion; 2) the burden on the patient of having to carry the analyst's unconscious sexuality recreates the pathogenic parent-child relationship which is more likely to deepen rather than heal the incest wound.

Having practiced as a physician for a number of years before I became an analyst, I am familiar with the detachment which is required of the physician in relationship to a patient. The physician must train to remain emotionally detached when examining and treating naked patients. Surely, the patient who stands naked and vulnerable before a physician has a right to expect that his or her body will not be harmed or violated. Similarly, this same medical model has been transferred to the psychotherapeutic situation, where the patient is supposed to expose a naked and vulnerable soul. But soul healing may require different approaches and principles, particularly where the wounds to the soul are in the areas of love and sex, and mind/body splitting. I will attempt to show that the soul connection between analyst and analysand is central to the healing process—and this is not possible unless the analyst is also willing and able to reveal his or her own soul.

Perhaps even with the physician, the detachment which he assumes in relationship to the naked body is not really essential. Is it perhaps only another manifestation of the Cartesian distrust and fear of our animal instinctual nature? I think so. And it has led to a totally mechanistic philosophy of medicine in which the body is viewed as nothing but a soulless machine consisting of its various moving parts, requiring a super specialist to treat each part. I do not believe scientific objectivity and emotional detachment is what really protects the patient from bodily harm by the physician. Rather, the very nature of the therapeutic situation evokes protective instincts toward the exposed and vulnerable person. Even among animals, as Lorenz has shown,[1] such instincts seem to exist. If anything, the cold distance imposed by scientific objectivity has resulted in the most terrible violations to the human body.

An important aspect of analytical work is the exploration and reevaluation of the patient's old attitudes (conscious and unconscious). Here the analyst functions more as a teacher than as a healer, and his own attitudes and values are bound to have a profound influence on the patient. The idea that the analyst functions as a spiritual guide and mentor, a guru, arises from this necessary aspect of the process. In Jungian analysis particularly, the role of the analyst as a *psychopomp*, the one who shows the way, is emphasized. Consequently, the Jungian school has tended to become a philosophical system concerned with the ethical, moral, and religious dilemma of modern humanity and has moved away from the more specifically therapeutic concerns of

---

1. Konrad Lorenz, Kin*g Solomons' Ring: New Light on Animal Ways*. New York: Crowell, 1952, 186 f.

psychopathology. Some of its practitioners have even questioned whether analytical psychology belongs in the tradition of the healing arts. Although psychoanalysts theoretically are more concerned with pathology, in practice their methods are also largely educational. Their basic assumptions, not unlike the Jungians, are that through making conscious the unconscious, new ego attitudes develop which help free the individual from the oppressive grip of the pathogenic complex. Of course, the analyst's values and philosophical orientation carry considerable weight in determining the direction which the patient's new ego attitudes take; even if the analyst's standards are not overt and expressed, he is there as a model by virtue of his role. Be that as it may, the assumption is that the patient's repressed instinctual complex will be healed through this process. In practice, however, a change in ego attitude, an awareness and acceptance of the unconscious complex, has proven more often than not to be inadequate in effecting a change or healing. This has been accounted for in two ways: either there has been only an intellectual realization and acceptance, or the realization has not been dealt with in the transference situation—a situation where an individual transfers a repressed experience from the past onto a relationship in the present. No doubt there is some truth in these explanations. But one may question this hypothesis since there have been enough instances where the acceptance has been not only intellectual, where the complex has been dealt within the transference situation, and still no healing of the instinct has occurred.

Do we have any knowledge, any psychological laws available that can lead us to more adequate methods of healing our sick animal-instinctual nature? I think we do. We know, for example, that the neglect, abuse, oppression, and repression of our instincts is largely responsible for their present abused condition. Like any other mistreated living creature, they have become misshapen and injured in their development; they are now weak, helpless, servile, or angry and sadistically aggressive. As our society has moved progressively toward computer control and mechanization, these instincts have been forced to flee to hidden chambers of our being. They have become like hunted animals—untamed and wild, fearful and cut off from the human condition. As for those instincts which have stayed, they have lost their vitality and have had to submit to the robot-brained orders of their once human masters.

But our humanness is dependent on our animal vitality and warmth. Paradoxically, the animal nature in us needs the warmblooded embrace and sympathetic human connection in order to be healed, and this cannot occur without the help of the animals themselves. This is the difficulty. It is as if we must submit to our now unreliable and dangerously neglected animal instincts so that their vital warmth can reenter our souls before we become capable of giving them what they need.

It is difficult, indeed. Do we dare put our faith and trust in sick, misshapen, vicious, and perhaps monstrous aspects of our being? Perhaps the idea will not seem so threatening and impossible if we remember that this is a common motif in fairy tales. Often the redemption of the hero is totally dependent on his trusting or befriending a dangerous, repulsive, or apparently insignificant animal. Still, it is not without danger. One must make certain preparations, meet certain preparations, meet certain conditions, and receive protective blessings and sanctification from higher powers, before one is ready to undertake the journey. I believe the analytical ritual can fulfill these preconditions and requirements so that when the time comes to trust the animal, one is already in a better relationship to it, and it is no longer as threatening or dangerous as it once was.

When one is able to submit to the analytical discipline and ritual—and bear in mind that many are not able to—the major part of the work involves bringing the animals and other aspects of the personality out of their hidden chambers in the unconscious. This generally has a salutary effect in itself. The animals seem to become gradually more friendly and appealing: this can be seen in the changes which occur in dreams. Unquestionably, the animals must sense or know that some effort is finally being made to help them. In addition, when the analyst has a good relationship to his or her instincts, the human warmth and sympathy toward the patient's frustrated and suffering animals helps to transform some of their fear and anger toward the human condition. But real healing and transformation cannot occur until the patient is ready and able to trust to their help and guidance and to relinquish the oppressive control which the rational mind has had over them. The patient, however, can go no further in his or her development and healing than the analyst has gone. So the analyst as well as the patient must gain the courage to trust *animal nature*.

The animal does not ultimately get healed through instinctual gratification, but through being able to enter into a warm and living connection with the spiritual essence of man. What assurance is there then that the animal will not go against its greater needs if we submit to it? None, really. But the long preparation necessary in the analytical work before one is even ready to submit, effects certain definite changes in the animal which decrease the likelihood of this occurring. For example, one may have no inhibitions about gratifying the sexual instinct, but this does not necessarily mean the instinct is healthy. It is in fact essential that this instinct, like all instincts, be restrained and regulated so that it can become gradually humanized. During the analytical work, with individuals who have had no apparent moral restrictions on their sexual activity, it seems the instinct itself begins to realize that restraint is necessary if it is to become human. In my practice I have seen considerable evidence of this in the body's reactions and in dreams. For example, a woman's vagina will suddenly close up and resist all her efforts to open for intercourse; in dreams, animals often speak and inform the dreamer of their need for human warmth and love, rather than sexual gratification.

On the other hand, something else occurs with individuals who have been inhibited and fearful of their sexuality. It seems that it is not only the ego or superego which is causing the sexual difficulties, but that other forces have been at work restraining the animal. When such an individual becomes aware of the need to satisfy sexual desires, often he or she finds it extremely difficult to do so in spite of the changes which have occurred in their conscious attitudes. He or she may try, but some form of impotency, frigidity, or blockage frequently makes it impossible or unsatisfactory. One often discovers during analytical work that the soul, or that power which is moving the individual toward wholeness, has been restraining the animal. Conscious awareness of this fact makes it possible to submit to the animal with some assurance that it will not settle for mere instinctual gratification.

On the other hand something else occurs with individuals who have been inhibited and fearful of their sexuality. It seems that it is not only the ego or superego which is causing the sexual difliculties, but that other forces have been at work restraining the animal. When such an individual becomes aware of the need to satisfy sexual desires, the person often finds it difficult to do so in spite of the changes which have occurred in one's conscious attitudes. They may try, but some form of impotency, frigidity, or blockage frequently makes it impossible or unsatisfactory. One often discovers during the analytical work that the soul, or that power which is moving the individual toward wholeness, has been restraining the animal. Conscious awareness of this fact makes it possible to submit to the animal with some assurance that it will not settle for mere instinctual gratification.

The fear of surrendering to our animal instinctual nature is intimately related to the fear of losing rational control of oneself. This in turn is related to a distrust of the spontaneous expressions of our being when these instincts are no longer under the control of the rational mind.

The rational mind—ego consciousness—functions as a mediating instrument between inner and outer reality. There is always a danger of transgressing collectively acceptable modes of behavior when a center other than ego consciousness is allowed to take over. The four basic animal instinctual drives—hunger, sex, fight, and flight—can cause considerable embarrassment or danger or both, to the individual and others if they are not regulated by the rational mind. At least this would seem to be a fair statement of the case for the ego's resistance to relinquishing its control over our sensual nature. The fear is that all the highly-valued human virtues would soon disappear, and greed, avarice, lust, uninhibited fornication, cowardice and murder would become rampant.

Well we have for a long time allowed ourselves to be ruled by the god of reason, and such virtues as courage, love, human decency, and individuality would seem to be at their lowest ebb. Furthermore, despite human bias against untamed instinctual drives, studies of animal behavior clearly indicate that even the most savage animals are much more sensitive in their relationship to their fellows than we have previously acknowledged. Clearly we need to reevaluate our views and understanding of the animal instincts.

Since animals do not have a cultural tradition, we must assume that instinctual patterns are primarily responsible for the regulation of animal relationships. One of the most important functions of the rational mind is the passing down of ritual, custom, and tradition from one generation to another. Children need to be instructed and indoctrinated into the patterns of their culture, and many primitive rituals are designed for this purpose.

We know that animals express a certain amount of restraint, ritual, or even "manners," in their eating and feeding habits, in their expressions of love, sex, and aggression, and in their respect for the territorial, and possibly, seniority rights of their species. However when two animals are drawn sexually towards each other, there does not seem to be any instinctual pattern of restraint or inhibition that obstructs the fulfillment of the drive. So far as we know, there is no taboo against sexual relations between parent and child, brother and sister, and so forth among animals. A more powerful adversary or a conflict of instincts might inhibit the sexual drive in an animal, but there is no evidence in the animal kingdom of anything like the incest taboo, the menstrual taboo, the masturbation taboo, and the rules governing sexual fidelity in marriage.

The sexual life of animals seems to be regulated and ritualized by biological rhythms and instinctual patterns. In humans the sexual drive is universally restricted by whatever a particular culture considers incestuous, as well as what is considered traditionally acceptable behavior in premarital and post-marital sexuality. The sexual drive in people, therefore, would appear to be modified by extrinsic factors belonging to culture rather than by nature.

It is difficult to conceive of people who would willingly allow the lower centers of body consciousness to regulate the ebb and flow of their human relationships if they believed that their nature, freed from ego control, would surely result in a transgression against their society. However I believe this fear is based on a gross misunderstanding of human nature. It does not take into account the historical evolution of human instincts and the transformations which occur in individual development, whereby the instincts are not necessarily in opposition to cultural values.

Ego consciousness functions largely as the observing mind's eye, which tends to increase the distance between subject and object. *Body consciousness,* on the other hand, draws one into an immediate and direct contact with another person or with an object. Modem humanity's fear and distrust of physical-sensual being are largely responsible for a sense of isolation and alienation. As long as humanity's spiritual and animal natures are not harmoniously in tune, the submission of one to the authority of the other will result in a splitting of the personality—a loss of the essential unity and wholeness of being. Ego consciousness functions as the carrier of cultural values and introduces the *objective* viewpoint into the *subjective* intra-psychic interplay within the individual. When there is a severe conflict between the unique spirit of individuals and the ethical and spiritual values of their culture, the ego tends to stand in the way of union between the spirit and the flesh. This is essentially the condition in which modern people find themselves. And there is no possibility of regaining wholeness until the rational mind is able to grasp and incorporate a new objective attitude, a set of values which is in essential agreement with the unique direction and strivings of the individual spirit. Thus the *ultimate* reconciliation *of the mind/body split* can *follow* only in *the wake of a gradual* continuing change in *the* conscious orientation and *attitudes of* the ego.

PSYCHOTHERAPY: FREUD AND JUNG

These days, when we speak of a person's morals, we tend to think immediately of their sexual morals. This is understandable when we consider how essential the regulation of the sexual instinct is for psychological and cultural development. The problem is, that aside from the rigid dogma of certain Protestant and fundamentalist sects, most of us live in a state of doubt and confusion about the meaning and nature of chaste and sinful sexuality. We know how psychologically and spiritually damaging it is to repress sexual desire, but we also know that complete sexual license can be equally damaging. If virtue and morality are so intimately related to the regulation of the sexual instinct, then we do indeed need to arrive at a new sexual morality.

Although many psychotherapists have moved away from Freud's dogmatic ideas on sexuality and tend to recognize other equally important factors as being responsible for psychic disturbances, the exposure and exploration of the vicissitudes of the sexual instinct are still central for several reasons. We have already indicated that the moral dilemma of modern humanity cannot be resolved until one is able to come to a new relationship to sexuality. The despair and meaningless suffering which afflicts modern humans is primarily due to a disturbed relationship to instinctual-emotional life. One has become estranged from the living quality of bodily existence because one has come to fear the spontaneity of sensual nature. The origins of this distrust, I believe, are found in guilt, fear, neglect, abuse, denigration, and rejection of an instinctual sexuality. Both the instinct itself and a relationship to it have been damaged, and the instinctual life has become contaminated by this distrust. Thus the healing of the sexual instinct is essential before a new harmony can be established between body and spirit.

The analytical ritual must be able to effect a significant increase in the basic harmony between the individual's spiritual and sensual nature, or it fails in its purpose. We know also that a healthier relationship to sexuality has a salutary effect on the totality of one's instinctual life. So it would seem that Freud may have been right after all: heal the sexual wounds and heal or make whole the person.

13

Still it seems to me that psychoanalysis has largely failed in its healing task. The limitations of Freud's biological orientation to sexuality and the human psyche, as well as the mechanistic development of his school are perhaps primarily responsible for this failure. It is unfortunate that Freud was not able to move towards the larger spiritual base on which Jung developed his school of analytical psychology because, it seems to me, humanity's relationship to instincts is a spiritual and religious issue which cannot be resolved within a purely mechanistic *Weltanschauung*.

On the other hand Jung might have bitten off more than he or his followers could chew, in that his system also tends to perpetuate a spirit/nature antithesis. Jung was primarily concerned with helping the individual reconnect to religious roots. For modern people this means moving away from an ego-centered base toward a living relationship with the higher authority and wisdom of the Self, or the God within. In making modern people aware of the limitations and destructiveness of his one-sided reliance on ego-consciousness, Jung will ultimately have as great an influence (if he has not already) as Freud has had with his explorations of sexuality. But the rational mind will never relinquish its position of control to the higher authority of the Self so long as one fears the spontaneous reactions of the Self's animal-sensual nature.

Jung's emphasis on the spiritual connection between analyst and analysand makes it extremely difficult to explore sexuality thoroughly. This is so because as soon as the analyst leaves an objective position and bares the soul in an authentic communion with a patient, the exploration of sexuality becomes much more charged and numinous. This situation is largely responsible for the tendency among Jungian analysts to avoid detailed discussion of sexual matters. Consequently the sexuality tends to get suppressed and spiritualized.

Psychoanalysts, on the other hand, because they try to remain objective and avoid involvement, are much better able to go into detailed discussion of sexual material. The discussion in such a laboratory atmosphere is much less charged and tends to be more matter of fact, generally. But in my opinion this is primarily why it fails to bring about any fundamental change and humanization of the sexual instinct. The healing of a wounded and mishapen instinct cannot occur apart from the human connection.

CHAPTER TWO

Soul, Instinct, Archetype, and Ego

Since the idea of soul is essential for any understanding of human experience, let me try to describe what I understand it to be. I have been sitting at my typewriter for some time, trying to start my description without much success. But I have been experiencing a continual flux of bodily sensations, feelings, emotions, ideas, images; anyone observing me in my relatively immobile state, would have no idea about what is going on inside of me. It is not possible to prove, to objectively verify, any of the things I am experiencing. They exist as a reality only for me. Yet my whole sense of being alive is dependent on what I am experiencing inside. I have no awareness or connection, at this instant, to anything on the outside. The quick of life, circulating throughout my body in ever-changing forms, is meaningful and important only to me. I do not know from moment to moment what impulse, sensation, feeling, image, or thought I will have.

My individual experience of the movements of a living pulse, a vital, ever-changing energy within my body, is what I understand as soul. (It is this unpredictable quality of soul, along with the fact that its existence cannot be objectively verified, that has put the word into such disfavor in our scientifically oriented world.)

My ego, my rational mind, has the capacity to detach itself from my body, to sever or block out its connection to my soul. But a healthy ego functions primarily to mediate between the soul (inner reality) and outer reality. It is a storehouse of information and conclusions drawn from past experience. It has the capacity to evaluate critically and to sort information. The soul needs the ego in order to develop and shape itself, and the ego needs the life-giving connection to the soul or it becomes only a sterile, rigid accumulation of past facts, opinions and experiences. If I habitually close myself to the spontaneous movements of my soul, I will become rigid and mechanical, more and more robot-like as the years pass. I will become a prisoner of calcified values and opinions, incapable of experiencing the renewal of life which the soul brings.

My connection to my own soul, therefore, depends on this ego-soul relationship. The vital moving force within us is soul, spirit, or whatever we choose to call it. Whatever it is, it is not ego. The ego can only move us in a mechanical, predictable fashion, which lacks the spontaneous living quality of a soul-directed individual. When the black man accuses the white man of lacking soul, he is saying that white men are caught within the narrow confines of rigid ego patterns, that they are not open to and in tune with the irrational movements of the life force.

Many factors have entered into Western culture's neglect and fear of soul. The most obvious is the belief that reason is the directing intelligence, the supreme authority, the prime mover: humans alone are guided by reason, all other creatures are guided by instinct. This attitude which holds instinct as something inferior and belonging to animals, as something to be overcome and replaced by reason, reflects very much the same attitude which Western man has come to have toward his soul. There is a direct relationship between man's attitude toward his instincts, and his attitude toward his soul.

There is an equally important question: What about man's connection to the soul of another? If he is cut off from his own soul, he will surely experience difficulty having a soul-connection with another person because the same ego obstructions are at work. (Analysis, incidently, is primarily concerned with helping the individual reestablish a connection to his own soul. It is assumed that the connection to others will improve through this process. While this is generally true, it does not happen automatically because soul-connection—to oneself or to another—demands care and cultivation). When I am having a warm, sensual, and loving connection with my own soul, there is an open channel of communication between my ego and my soul—not the slightest barrier is in the way. When I experience a soul-connection to another, it has this same quality: there must be an open channel—for, if there is the slightest barrier, no real contact, no interchange of soul-substance can occur.

Now this downgrading of the experiences of inner reality has had a paradoxical, but psychologically predictable, effect on modern man, namely, that it has resulted in an obsessive preoccupation with oneself, and a relative lack of connection to objects or people outside of oneself. In other words, the neglected inner experiences and images have grabbed us from behind, so to speak, and we literally have enormous difficulties distinguishing inside from outside. Particularly in any prolonged relationship, such as marriage, we tend to bore our spouses because of our self preoccupations. In addition, knowingly or unknowingly we tend to burden our wives or husbands with the demand to take care of our own neglected soul. A great deal of the frustrating dissatisfactions, the lack of communication, the disharmony in relationships, is caused by this lack of soul-connection.

I

Current behavior theories all start from the premise that instincts originate in the physical structure of the organism, in a specific neural pattern or structure. This view dominates psychology, as well as the natural and behavioral sciences. It results in a mechanistic philosophy of man and life. Jung's theory of the archetypes, following in the Vitalist tradition, reintroduces the ancient idea that a nonmaterial force or principle animates and directs all living organisms. It is not surprising, therefore, that there has been so little understanding or acceptance of Jung's archetypal theory among psychologists and scientists. Freud, on the other hand, clearly locates the origins of the instincts in the somatic organization of the organism.

What are the implications of these opposing views regarding the origin and nature of instincts? How do they effect one's attitude and understanding of life's processes and the human condition? How do they influence the path one takes toward psychic development and wholeness?

In Freud's mechanistic view, as we have seen, consciousness and psychic life are believed to have their origins in the physical and chemical structure of the organism. The instincts function entirely to gratify, to relieve the somatic tensions of the organism; this applies equally to man and animal. According to this theory, only with the emergence of a mental function (the ego) from the instinctual substrata, does a specifically human quality begin to develop through learning experiences. The ego is thus defined as a mental function which acts as an intermediary between the instincts (id) and the external world. The uniquely human qualities and development of the individual are conceived as being entirely dependent on external influences and an adequately functioning ego.[1] The idea that there are inborn, inherited transcendent forms (archetypes) which are capable of releasing uniquely human instinctual patterns of thought and behavior, has no place in such a system.

A somatic theory of instincts must lead to an ego-centered psychology. In Freud's system, it is entirely up to the ego to regulate and direct the flow of psychic energies, to mediate between id and superego, inner and outer reality. Thus the ego is *the* individualizing and humanizing factor within the human personality.

This is hard to believe. There is nothing particularly individual about anyone's ego, nor is there anything particularly appealing about the ego. One may be momentarily impressed by a brilliant display of ego virtuosity, but it soon becomes a bore. It lacks all the substantial qualities which are attractive and humanly appealing. The ego is really rather empty and lifeless. It only becomes alive and beautiful when it is serving something other than itself.

The fact that an instinct manifests itself in the somatic structure of an organism, creating physiological tensions which provoke certain typical patterns of behavior, is no proof that an instinctual reaction is

---

1. Sigmund Freud, *An Outline of Psychoanalysis*, London: Hogarth Press, 1955, 23.

purely the result of biological processes. A critical reevaluation of this view is needed, since it is the basis upon which most current instinct theories rest.

II

Let us begin by examining the generally accepted view of the relationship between instinct and emotion: physiological changes, it is believed, produce the emotion which always accompanies an instinctual reaction. As William James put it, "We feel sorry because we cry, angry because we strike, afraid because we tremble, and not that we cry, strike, or tremble, because we are sorry, angry, or fearful, as the case may be."[2] This theory about the relationship between instinct and emotion does not stand the test of empirical observations, yet it is rarely questioned by most animal and human investigators. One often experiences all the physiological components of an instinctual reaction without necessarily experiencing the feelings and emotions which typically accompany the instinct. Let me demonstrate this by two examples: 1) one may experience all the physical changes that occur with the stimulation of the hunger instinct without having any real emotional desire for food; 2) one may experience all the physiological changes which occur with sexual arousal without having any urge or need for sexual gratification. Such observations suggest that the emotional impetus or drive behind an instinctual reaction is not bound to the neurophysiological mechanisms of the organism, that it may originate from another source. It also suggests that the directing and driving energy behind an instinctual reaction transcends the physical-chemical structure and mechanisms of the body.

An instinct-releasing stimulus, internal or external, must evoke a mental image as well as a physical response in the organism. An instinctual reaction occurs when there is an unobstructed flow of energy between the image and the bodily reaction, when the psyche and some

_____

2. William James, *Principles of Psychology*, Vol. II, New York: Dover Publications, 1950, 450.

of the organism are unified in a total response. The mental image alone is no more capable of releasing the instinct than are the physiological changes and tensions. To reverse our two examples, one may have an image of a desirable food or desired sexual object, but without the corresponding bodily changes there is no emotion. It would seem, therefore, that the emotional force or drive necessary for the release of an instinct depends upon the simultaneous occurrence of the psychic and physical manifestations of the instinct; and, as stated above, an unobstructed connection between them.

Since we have shown that either the mental or bodily component of an instinct can occur without necessarily evoking the other, it appears that they are not causally related even though they are two halves of a totality. We must also conclude that emotions do not necessarily have a somatic or psychic origin. In addition, Freud's idea that mental life originates in the somatic organization of the individual becomes untenable.

All we can say empirically about the origins of the emotional drive behind an instinct is that it becomes manifest only when there is a conjunction between the mental image and the bodily reaction. Although it is possible to focus on the mental image and eventually evoke the missing bodily reaction and emotion, and vice versa, it is not inevitable (i.e., one may be able to produce sexual arousal and desire by meditating upon sexual images and fantasies, but one cannot predict that a physical response will necessarily occur). Our egos can not cause the simultaneous occurrence of the mental and physical components of the instinct, nor can they effect their union. What, then, is responsible? Where is the source of the Desire, the Will which directs, controls, and releases the instinctual reaction?

III

If I understand Jung's view regarding the relationship between instinct and archetype it is essentially as follows: the archetype can manifest itself either in a physical reaction or in a mental representation or image; Jung considers the archetypal image to be the mental representation of the instinct; in addition, he states, "It is impossible to say which comes first—apprehension of the situation, or the impulse to act."[3] I agree generally, but I do not think Jung has given sufficient attention to the precise relationship between the physical and psychic components of the instinct. In many places, for example, he refers to the instinctual reaction as belonging to one category and the mental image as belonging to another. He uses the term instinctual reaction to designate the physiological and physical response of the organism. This is inaccurate, because the evidence suggests that an instinctual pattern of reaction occurs only when the physical and psychic components of the instinct are joined. The simultaneous occurrence of an internal image of a desirable object is necessary in order to release the instinct. If there is not a strong, definite feeling or emotion to move toward or away from a specific object, the impetus to act upon the physical or mental component of the instinct is lacking. *Thus the driving and directing force behind an instinct is contained in an emotion.* The origin of this emotion is unknown. It is inaccurate to postulate either that the physical reactions of the organism cause the emotion or that it arises from the mental image or representation. The mental and physical components of an instinct do not always appear hand in hand, nor do they necessarily have to follow one upon the other; when they appear separately, there is no emotion and consequently no instinctual reaction.

Perhaps the emotion simply arises out of the simultaneous appearance and conjunction of the psyche and soma. However, this concept leaves us still in the dark about the cause of this simultaneous appearance and conjunction of the instinctual components. Such a concept would be of enormous value in understanding more about the nature of the mind/body split and the processes involved in healing the split.

---

3. C. G. Jung, "Instinct and The Unconscious," *CW 8*, New York: Pantheon Books, 1960, 282.

Empirical evidence suggests that the directing drive contained in the emotion is antecedent, and transcendent to the physical and psychic manifestations of the instinct, and that it is also responsible for their conjunction. From this view, it follows that emotion and feeling contain a vital energy which is both the prime mover and the directing intelligence in all sentient beings. It leads us away from the current view that it is man's intellect and reason which should direct his actions. Without an emotion behind it, the rational mind becomes impotent and incompetent. Emotion is the sacred channel through which a directing intelligence enters the soul.

IV

There are some conceptual ambiguities in Jung's theory of the archetypes which tend to obscure and undermine the basic soundness of his ideas. His view, as I understand it, is that the dynamism of instinct is biologically rooted and that the apprehension of the instinct in the form of psychic images and ideas is a function of the archetype. "Archetype and instinct are the most polar opposites imaginable, as can easily be seen when one compares a man who is ruled by his instinctual drives with a man who is seized by the spirit."[4] Thus, Jung seems to be in essential agreement with the biologically oriented instinct theories so far as instinctual patterns of behavior are concerned, but he derives the psychic component of the instinct from inherited psychic dispositions or form-principles, the archetypes. I say "seems" because in other places he suggests that instinct and archetype may be identical.[5] And in still another place, he suggest that instinct may be derived from an archetype.[6]

This basic difficulty could be cleared up if we stopped thinking of instinct and archetypal image as a pair of opposites. An instinctual reaction is always the result of a combination of specific physical reactions of the organism with corresponding psychic images. It is therefore not instinct and image which form a pair of opposites, but the somatic and psychic manifestations of the instinct which result in an instinctual reaction when they are united. With this formulation,

24

the archetype is viewed as both the carrier and the source of instinct, as the directing and unifying force or principle behind the physical patterns and the mental representations of the instinct. It would also support two possibilities that Jung has suggested: 1) that instinct is derived from an archetype; 2) that spirit and matter meet in the archetype.

Jung's idea of opposites has led him to some other conclusions which need examination. He has accepted the idea of a spirit/instinct antithesis[7] which does not exist when the archetype is conceived as being the carrier of instinct. As a consequence, Jung, following Janet, views the instincts as the *partie inferieure,* and the psyche as the *partie superieure.*[8] This view tends to increase the split between spirit and nature and obstructs the individuation process. It elevates the psyche and devaluates the bodily component of the instinct: Ego consciousness, free will, and psychological development then become solely a function of mental images and processes; the dialectical relationship between the ego and internal images becomes the only true and trusted path for the spiritualization of blind, compulsive, instinctual patterns of reaction; strong emotions, which are always linked to an instinct, become suspect and tend to be used by the ego only for increasing consciousness when one functions within this system; the emotional centers of bodily consciousness cannot be trusted as a spiritual guide and principle; the ego must separate, detach itself from instinct in order to effect a transformation. This view tends ultimately to lead right back to the ego as the humanizing and transforming instrument of the human personality—which is not what Jung meant to do at all. Although Jung states that an archetype is the authentic *spiritus rector*[9] behind the human ego or intellect, this becomes mere theory if instinct is experienced as being in opposition to psychological development. To further complicate matters, Jung has frequently proposed the existence

4. C. G. Jung, "On The Nature of the Psyche," *CW 8*, New York: Pantheon Books, 1960, §406.

5. *Ibid.,* §404.

6. *Ibid.,* §416.

7. *Ibid.,* §407.

8. *Ibid.,* §375.

of a spiritual or individuating instinct in man.

An individual's physical and psychological development is a function of an internal guiding and directing principle (the archetype); it moves (through emotion) the individual always toward completion and therefore is to be trusted whether or not its purpose is consciously apprehended; this archetype is the source of the human instincts. What, then, is the function of the human ego? What is the relationship between ego consciousness and psychological development? Can the instinct (archetype) alone be trusted as a guide toward individuation? If so, why do so many humans remain unconscious and undeveloped all their lives?

V

There can be no psychological development without a continual expansion of ego consciousness; nor is individuation possible without a dialectical relationship between ego and unconscious, ego and soul. Nevertheless, the development of consciousness is neither the path nor the goal of psychological development—ego consciousness is only a necessary prerequisite. What is crucial is the ego's mediating position between the archetypes and external reality: its capacity to inform, restrain and contain the powerful thrust of the archetype in order to give the soul time to effect a reconciliation between inner and outer reality. Individuation is a continual process of making whole, of creating new unities. That is why the concept of instinct is so central: *Only an instinct is capable of unifying the whole man so that he responds with his totality.*

So long as ego consciousness and the *psyche* are considered to be superior functions responsible for spiritual development, and the instincts are viewed simply as relatively unalterable, automatic functions which play little or no part in promoting psychological transformation, the individual becomes mistrustful of the very function that is truly responsible for individuation. And it does not help matters

---

9. Jung, *CW 8*, §406.

when Jung proposes that there is an individuating instinct which can be trusted to direct the soul's development, because how is one to differentiate between our so-called animal instinctual nature and our spiritualizing instinct? Every analyst knows, or should know, that a powerful primitive emotion can effect an authentic psychological transformation if it is trusted, just as often as can a great spiritual revelation.

Jung left his ideas about the relationship between ego and instinct in a very loose and ambiguous state, which circumstance has served to weaken his great contributions concerning the relationship between ego and Self,[10] and the nature and function of the religious attitude. As a consequence, his followers tend to fall into a "piousity" which lacks the strength and vitality of the authentic religious function; or, they tend to end up once again with the ego-Self identity. Of course, his opponents can, with some justification, write off his ideas as mystical mumbojumbo or Jungian *schwammerei.* I believe the future of analytical psychology as a creative instrument for healing Western man's spiritual collapse is largely dependent on the clarification and development of Jung's concepts on the relationship between ego and instinct.

I feel that the soul is the directing intelligence and energy which shapes the life and fate of the individual; that it is experienced as a force which always moves toward unification of psyche and soma, and inner and outer reality; and that this unifying action is of the nature of an instinct and can therefore not be differentiated from any other instinct. The goal of the soul is wholeness, the continual creation of new unities. The development of consciousness is but an instrument in the process of creative transformation, not the goal of individuation. Thus, consciousness is always threatened by the instinctual actions of the soul when it distrusts or denies the creative validity of an instinctual surge of energy and emotion. If ego and instinct are in opposition, if they are not united in their goals, then the ego loses its connection to that which is most vital to the creative unfolding of the personality. Thus, even ego consciousness is dependent on a trust in the superior

27

guiding action of the instincts. The psyche, in my opinion, is not the *partie superieure* as Jung has at times suggested.

VI

The aim of the analytical process might be stated as follows: to help the individual regain his trust and connection to his instincts, so that he may live spontaneously, instinctually and creatively. An animal lives its entire life this way, and so can a very unconscious human. Is this, then, the goal of the process? No. Consciousness, as I have indicated, is an essential ingredient in the process of psychological development. But it is the creative role and function of ego consciousness which needs clarification—the ego's relationship to the instincts.

The critical creative functions of the ego are differentiation, mediation, and its capacity to restrain and contain the powerful thrust of the instinctual drive. A separation between the physical and psychic components of the instinct is caused by the latter function, and this in turn is responsible for stimulating the uniquely human flow of images and imaginative activity. It is because the psyche carries the highest human values and aspirations that it has been elevated above the instincts, but let us not forget that mental activity is as much a manifestation of the instinct as are physical reactions.

Now, when the ego resists the immediate release of an instinctual drive, it finds itself caught between the physical and psychic components of the instinct. For example, when the ego does not allow the body to act upon a sexual desire, the instinctual energy is temporarily diverted into the psychic realm where it expresses itself in a variety of images and ideas. These mental representations are in

---

10. Jung uses the term Self to refer to the totality of the personality—conscious and unconscious, ego and non-ego. Throughout this book I will use the terms Self and soul interchangeably. As I have indicated, the ego is a function of the soul which is capable of detaching itself; thus one can speak of a relationship between ego and soul, or ego and Self.

turn able to evoke feelings which transcend the original aim of the instinct: tenderness, companionship, love, the need for a permanent mate, the need to raise a family, power, and prestige. This is not to say that the original aim of the instinct is lost. When the ego functions creatively, it is able to maintain a connection between the physical and spiritual aims of the instinct. Even though it is responsible for the separation, it also functions as a mediator. In addition, the ego has information concerning external reality which the instinct may not have; here, too, it functions as a mediator. However, the creative resolution of this tension between the spiritual and animal (biological) portions of the instinct, between internal and external reality, is a function of instinct, not the ego. Whenever the ego attempts to resolve the conflict, it ends up by moving towards one pole of the opposition at the expense of the other: i.e., spirit over matter or vice versa, external over internal reality or vice versa. The transforming function of the instinct cannot effect a unification of the opposites so long as the ego distrusts and fears the animal-sensual portion of the soul. One never knows through which instinctual channel the soul will choose to perform its reconciling function; thus it is potentially obstructive to psychological transformation for the ego to establish a hierarchy of spirit over matter, or one instinct over another.

Psychology has come to identify the function of consciousness with the ego. I think this is a mistake which has led to an inadequate understanding of ego function. There are many centers of consciousness within the body which can function independently of the ego. Every cell, every organ, has an awareness which makes it capable of responding appropriately to stimuli independent of the higher cortical functions and the ego. The ego is a specialized function of consciousness which is most highly developed in man. Above all, it gives man a sense of the location and limits of his being in time and space. All other forms of consciousness transcend the space-time continuum. Ego-consciousness is, therefore, the essential instrument for mediating between the inner timeless world and outer reality.

During a period when the ego is critically sorting and evaluating

29

the information it is receiving from within and without, only limited action is possible. Decisive action of any kind, aside from habitual mechanical types of actions, cannot occur so long as the ego is in control. Thus, an immediate and spontaneous reaction is never ego-directed. The ego is not the directing energy and intelligence in the human personality. It functions essentially like a computer memory bank, giving information and even opinions, but the final decision is always in the hand of that greater Will which moves us. It is a fantastic delusion to believe that our rational mind directs our lives.

PART TWO

Incest

What of this eternal longing for wholeness? Is it not the need to return to the childhood state of bliss where mother responds to the child's cry of distress with instinctive knowledge and compassion? Though the child knows not what it needs, mother knows; and even though the child cries not, she knows. She knows everything! She is the all-knowing, all-powerful, all-nourishing, all-wise, all-loving MOTHER.

The longing to return to this idyllic state is fortunately resisted by the spirit. For, to find concrete fulfillment of this need means death to the spirit; an end to individuality. This is one reason why the violation of the incest taboo is such a terrible crime. Nevertheless, the man whose spirit aspires to the highest rung on the ladder, finds the gravitational pull toward concrete fulfillment becoming increasingly forceful as he laboriously reaches upward. Thus, says Kazantzakis, "The ancient, unrelenting and merciless battle between the spirit and the flesh has been the arena into which all men of the spirit, from time immemorial, have thrown themselves. I have fought to reconcile these two primordial forces which are so contrary to each other, to make them realize that they are not enemies but, rather, fellow workers, so that they might rejoice in their harmony—and so that I might rejoice with them."[1]

---

1. N. Kazantzakis, *The Last Temptation of Christ*, New York: Bantam Books, 1.

CHAPTER THREE

Incest and Wholeness

A s I begin this chapter, I suddenly feel the need to reconsider the value of my own long quest to attain wholeness. Is it really desirable for a person to attempt to reconcile the split within psyche? Is not the eternal opposition between mind and body, between spiritual and animal natures, the stuff out of which humanness flows? Should one undo the long process which has gradually separated humanity from instincts? Animals respond with their totality and wholeness because they live purely by instinct. Is my view that humanity must heal and redeem its animal nature in order to become whole again perhaps a regressive, romantic image of the "noble savage?" I do not think so, but I believe some discussion of these doubts is needed.

If I have implied that humanity can only find joy and meaning in life through wholeness, I must correct that notion. The states of being split and fragmented by opposites, imbalance, disharmony, are not necessarily meaningless nor joyless. Only when such states become static do joy and meaning disappear from the world. Such opposition within the soul can be creative if there is a struggle toward reconciliation, so long as it is believed that balance and harmony can be regained, that a new wholeness can be created. A person can realize and be fulfilled in this ebb and flow between separation and union, between disharmony and the creation of new wholes. I am concerned with the healing of the modern mind/body dichotomy because I believe that in too many people the separation has become static, causing a blockage of the stream of life, a situation which is *evil* and *sickness.* I do not see the healing of the split as leading to a permanent union of the two; rather, the goal is to restore the creative tension, a working partnership between the spiritual and animal portions of the soul.

On the other hand, when it comes to the human connection, inner unity and wholeness are essential. True union with another person is possible only if one's total being is available to connect with the other. The instincts which join one's totality to another cannot function naturally and spontaneously so long as the ego remains out of it, creating the situation of the detached observer. The rational mind must be able to surrender to the instincts if there is to be soul connection. Particularly in human relationships must one be able to trust the animal, to react spontaneously and instinctually. However, this does not mean that one must regress to an animal level of behavior in order to connect to another. Not at all. Human instincts are capable of change, development, and transformation.

The developmental process through which instincts gradually transform is perhaps best described as *psychisation:* that is, when an instinctual drive is inhibited, it tends to stimulate the formation of images which are the mental equivalents of the desired objects. The hunger instinct, for example, first manifests itself as a physiological reaction to the need for food—stomach contractions, salivation etc. If an acceptable food is immediately available, there is a direct discharge and gratification of the instinct. Images of specific desirable foods only begin to enter consciousness when the immediate discharge of the instinct is not possible. The formation of mental images and categories can thus be understood as psychic equivalents of physical reactions. This is essentially how Jung understands the *archetypal* image: namely, the psychic representation of an instinct. The archetype is an inherent disposition responsible for both the physical reaction and its psychic equivalent. In other words the latent structure of the archetype can become manifest in certain typical patterns of behavior or in equally typical mental images and constructs.

Humanity is unique largely because of imagination. A person promotes image formation and imaginative activity by restricting the direct and immediate gratification of one's animal nature. One is capable of enduring great sensual frustration and deprivation; but, if one is deprived of connection to meaningful dreams and images, if one has no hope of ever regaining them, a person cannot live. *The mystery surrounding the taboo against incest is directly related to the development of these internal images of union and wholeness.*

A sense of wholeness is dependent on images of the harmonious connection between the masculine and feminine opposites. This is fundamental to the human condition. Where such images are lacking or in perpetual opposition, the individual lives a fragmented existence, out of tune with oneself and with the basic harmony of the universe. The human instinct behind these images expresses itself in the form of symbols representing the union of opposites, such as: The Royal Marriage or *hierosgamos,* the Brother-Sister Incest archetype, the image of Romantic Love, the conjunction of Sun and Moon, Heaven and Earth, Spirit and Matter, Mind and Body, The Magic Circle or Mandala, etc.

Although the experience of the archetype of union is an inherent human disposition, it needs to be released by an external stimulus and experienced in its projected and incarnated form before it can be internalized. For a child, a crucial formative experience of this archetype is in its incarnation of the harmonious connection and interaction between mother and father; and through repeated experiences of its own wholeness in relationship to both parents. When the fundamental connection between husband and wife is obstructed, the child's formative experience of the archetype of the Royal Marriage is also obstructed. This is inevitable even if a surface harmony exists between the couple. In addition, when there is a lack

35

of spiritual harmony between mother and father, each parent tends to project the ideal of a soul-mate onto a child of the opposite sex. As a consequence, an unconscious spiritual marriage is formed between father and daughter, and mother and son. I believe this has been a prevailing pattern in our culture for a long time, and that it is largely responsible for the soul-splitting dichotomy between mind and body which afflicts modern people.

A child, like an animal, has an instinctual awareness of what is really happening in the emotional-feeling life of adults. For example a female child will sense when there is a stronger bond between herself and her father than between her mother and father. She has hardly left the cradle, and she is already plunged into the classical incestuous triangle! The taboo against incest is unquestionably part of humanity's psychic inheritance. Even if it is not yet functioning in early childhood, it is certainly experienced by the child in relationship to the parents. For the female child, the father is thus experienced very early as being in some way forbidden to her as physical object but not to the mother. As the child develops, her emerging sexuality causes a serious problem for her in relationship to father, which is usually resolved by a repression of the instinct. At the same time, of course, she is aware of having a stronger spiritual bond to father than mother has, which only increases the burden of her incest guilt. In spite of the underlying soul-mate bond between father and daughter, the child is unable to experience her wholeness in relationship to him because of the incestuous triangle. Her relationship to him becomes increasingly fragmented and frustrating as she matures. The same pattern occurs with a male child in relationship to his mother.

The psychological significance of the incest mystery seems to have been lost to modem people. I see little hope for change in the typical soul-splitting Oedipal or Electra syndrome described above, unless the existing forms of marriage, family, and community life are renewed through a new connection to the mystery of incest.

---

2. C. G. Jung, *Symbols of Transformation, CW 5*, London: Routledge, 1956, §332.

INCEST AND WHOLENESS

At the core of the incest problem is humanity's eternal longing to become whole again, to return to an original state of oneness before separation and duality were forced into existence by the birth of consciousness. But, as C. G. Jung puts it, "It is not the incestuous cohabitation that is desired, but rebirth."[2] The spirit of rebirth is what Otto calls the original religious spirit.[3] Then it follows that the universal existence of incest prohibitions and the religious impulse would appear to be closely related. The function of the incest taboo is to prevent the concretization of incest, for this would only lead to a regression. According to Jung, "The incest prohibition acts as an obstacle and makes the creative fantasy inventive; for instance, there are attempts to make the mother pregnant by means of fertility magic. The effect of the incest taboo and of the attempts at canalization is to stimulate the creative imagination, which gradually opens up possible avenues for the self realization of libido. In this way the libido becomes imperceptibly spiritualized."[4] Thus, if the flow of libido has become stuck in an incest complex, there would be an interference with the whole process of psychological development. The resolution of the Oedipus or Electra complex must therefore be a central therapeutic concern. However, for Jung, the incest desire is not something to be overcome or resolved, because it is the vehicle for psychological rebirth. Freud's reduction of the religious need to the Oedipus complex, and therefore something to be sublimated, reflects a different view. Furthermore considerable evidence exists that the Oedipal complex is not an essential phase of normal growth and development.

In Freud's view, part of the normal psychosexual development of a child involves the desire to have actual intercourse with the parent of the opposite sex. Empirical evidence accumulated in numerous case histories seems to support Freud's theory. Nevertheless I do not believe the incest taboo originates from a need to prevent sexual intercourse with the parents, though it is essential in discouraging intercourse

---

3. W. F. Otto, "The Meaning of the Elusinian Mysteries," in *The Mysteries* (*Eranos* 2), New York: Pantheon, 1955, 30.

4. Jung, *Symbols of Transformation*, §332.

between brother and sister. This is not to say that the child does not have sensuous desires toward the parents and that a child is not sexually aroused. When a child is overwhelmed with sexual desires toward a parent, it is generally provoked, consciously or unconsciously by a sexually disturbed parent. Only in such cases does one find the classical Oedipus complex as described by Freud.

The origins of the incest prohibition are unknown. Most theories attempt to establish biological or sociocultural causes for the existence of this taboo. Little attention has been paid to the idea that both the taboo and the desire for incest may have instinctual roots, that nature as well as culture is responsible for this uniquely human characteristic. This is understandable in Western civilization, since scientific materialism precludes the possibility that instincts have any role in the spiritual and cultural development of man. Reason alone is deemed responsible for human development. Humanity is unique only because it is capable of controlling instincts. How could anything so fundamental to the formation of the human family and society as the incest taboo possibly belong to an instinctual disposition? We will not labor this point, except to emphasize again that most investigations concerning the nature and meaning of incest have been under the domination of the anti-instinctual bias of Cartesian metaphysics.

The generally accepted premise is that in humanity cultural values and ideals have replaced instincts. Malinowski has described this process as being due to the plasticity of human instincts.[5] According to him the cultural mechanisms primarily responsible for this development are: 1) the taboos forbidding incest and adultery, 2) the cultural releases of the mating instinct, 3) the moral and ideal norms as well as the practical inducements which keep husband and wife together—the legal sanction of the marriage tie, 4) the dictates which shape and express parental tendencies.[6] Malinowski believes these cultural co-determinants closely follow the general course imposed by

5. Bronislaw Malinowski, *Sex and Repression in Savage Society*, New York: Meridian Books, 1955, 196.
6. *Ibid.*, 197.
7. Malinowski, *Sex and Repression*, 198.

nature on animal behavior, but he concludes that "the forces by which they shape human behavior are no longer *mere* instincts but habits into which man has been educated by tradition."[7]

Once again we see the Western prejudice against the instinctual. In this view instincts are fixed patterns of reaction to relatively specific, fixed stimuli. There is no room for the idea that instincts are capable of change and development, or that the stimulus which releases an instinct may also change.

I have already suggested that whenever an individual totally responds an instinct is always at work and that a strong emotion must be present in order for this to occur. It is most unlikely that any particular cultural value or institution could survive for long if it were not an expression of human instinctual need. Following this logic, the incest taboo and other forms of sexual restriction must be expressions of humanity's unique instinctual inheritance. Most social scientists view the incest taboo as a cultural invention necessary to preserve family unity and essential for the expansion of the family unit into larger cultural unities. While Malinowski does see the taboo as ultimately serving basic instinctual needs, i.e., the mating and parental instincts, he rejects the idea that the incest taboo could be an instinct.

There are, however, two schools of thought which do consider the incest taboo to be instinctual: 1) the biological theory that close inbreeding leads to a degenerate stock; 2) Westermark's[8] belief that prolonged intimacy within the family unit evokes an instinctual aversion to sexual contact. The evidence does not support either of these theories, and the contrary would, in fact, seem to be the case.

Whether or not the incest taboo is an instinct or a human invention would seem to make little difference. I would agree if its function was, as most social scientists believe, only to effect an harmonious structural organization of society. The mystery of incest has deep psychological significance, apart from social organization, which cannot even be considered or grasped unless the instinctual origins of the incest taboo are recognized. The tension between the incest desire

8. E. A. Westermark, *The History of Human Marriage*, London: Macmillan, 1908.

and incest prohibition seems to be essential for human psychological development. Repression of either the desire (as Freud, Malinowski and others suggest is essential for culture) or the prohibition is, in my opinion, obstructive to psychological growth. To understand this relationship, both the desire and the inhibition need to be viewed as aspects of one instinct.

How does the incest taboo function psychologically to promote human love and imagination? How does it set into motion the psychological humanization of a child? Let us begin our attempt to explain the nature of this process with an examination of primitive societies, where the incest taboo is still the active basis for social organization.

Exogamy, which is essentially an extension of the incest prohibition, is the principle upon which primitive societies are organized. In its simplest form the tribe is divided into two exogamous sections or phratries. Members of a particular phratry are considered 'brothers' and 'sisters' because of their common origins of descent: totemic, paternal, or maternal. Sex or marriage within the phratry is forbidden, but marriage outside of the tribe is also forbidden. Thus exogamy actually promotes a close kind of inbreeding even though it prohibits sex and marriage within the extended family unit.[9] We will not discuss the more complex kinship connections which occur when a tribe is divided into sub-phratries because the basic principle is the same.[10]

Kinship arrangements differ depending on whether the tribe bases descend on the mother (matrilineal) or on the father (patrilineal). Since the matrilineal system is more common in primitive societies, let us see how exogamy works in such cultures. With the Trobrianders of Melanesia "kinship" is reckoned through the mother only, and succession and inheritance descend in the female line. This means that the boy or girl belongs to the mother's family, clan and community: the

---

9. Ernest Crawly, *The Mystic Rose*, Vol. II, London: Methuen & Co. Ltd., 1927, 212-13.

10. For a detailed discussion of the phratry system and its relationship to the incest prohibition see: John Layard, *The Virgin Archetype*, New York: Spring Publications, 1972; also Crawly, and Malinowski, *The Sexual Life of Savages*.

11. Malinowski, *Sex and Repression*, 22.

boy succeeds to the dignities and social position of the mother's brother, and it is not from the father but from the maternal uncle or maternal aunt, respectively, that a child inherits its possessions.[11]

Matrimony is usually monogamous except with chiefs, who have several wives. A woman is believed to become pregnant from tiny spirits inserted into her womb, generally by the agency of the spirit of a deceased kinswoman of the mother. Her husband therefore is not regarded as father of the children, although he is expected to protect and cherish them when they are born. "The father is thus a beloved, benevolent friend, but not a recognized kinsman of the children . . . Real kinship, that is identity of substance, 'same body,' exists only through the mother. The authority over the children is vested in the mother's brother."[12] They are his heirs and successors, and he is also responsible for passing on to them the myths and traditions of the clan. He supplies his sister and her household with most of their food. Thus the mother's brother represents the principle of discipline, authority and executive power within the family, while the children look to the father only for love and companionship.[13]

> "Marriage is patrilocal: that is, the girl goes to join her husband in his house and migrates to his community, if she comes from another, which is in general the case. The children therefore grow up in a community where they are legally strangers, having no right to the soil, no lawful pride in the village glory; while their home, their traditional centre of local patriotism, their possessions, and their pride in their ancestors are in another place.
>
> "From an early age boys and girls of the same mother are separated in the family, owing to the strict taboo which enjoins them. Any subject connected with sex, above all, should never interest them in common. It thus comes about that though the brother is really the person in authority over the sister, the incest taboo forbids him to use this authority when it is a question of her marriage."[14]

---

12. Malinowski, *Sex and Repression*, 23.
13. *Ibid.*, 24.
14. *Ibid.*, 24.

Children are allowed complete freedom to explore their sexuality, except for the taboo between brother and sister.

> "From an early age, when the girl first puts on her grass petticoat, brothers and sisters of the same mother must be separated from each other, in obedience to the strict taboo which enjoins that there shall be no intimate relations between them. Even earlier, when they first can move about and walk, they play in different groups. Later on they never consort together socially on a free footing, and above all there must never be the slightest suspicion of an interest of one of them in the love affairs of the other. Although there is comparative freedom in playing and language between children, not even quite a small boy would associate sex with his sisters, still less make any sexual allusion or joke in their presence. This continues right through life, and it is the highest degree of bad form to speak to a brother about his sister's love affairs, or vice versa."[15]

The Trobrianders of Melanesia have no puberty initiation rites, but a partial breakup of the family occurs at this time because brother and sister can no longer reside in the same household. A boy must move to a special house which he shares with three to six other boys, who are joined by their sweethearts. He continues to live in such a house, the *bukumatula,* until he is married. While a girl continues to live at home, she too spends most of her nights with a lover in one *bukumatula* or another.[16]

The incest prohibition between brother and sister is the supreme taboo for the Trobriander.

> This taboo is the prototype of all that is ethically wrong and horrible to the native. It is the first moral rule seriously impressed in the individual's life, and the only one which is enforced to the full by all the machinery of social and moral sanctions. It is so deeply ingrained in the structure of native tradition that every individual is kept permanently alive to it.[17]

15. Malinowski, *Sex and Repression*, 58.
16. *Ibid.*, 66.
17. B. Mainowski, *The Sexual Life of Savages*, New York: Harcourt, Brace & World, 1929, 519.

42

INCEST AND WHOLENESS

Brother and sister thus grow up in a strange sort of domestic proximity: in close contact and yet without any personal or intimate communication; near to each other in space, near by rules of kinship and common interest; and yet, as regards personality, *always hidden and mysterious.* They must not even look at each other, they must never exchange any light remarks, never share their feelings and ideas. And as age advances and the other sex becomes more and more associated with love making, the brother and sister taboo becomes increasingly stringent. Thus, to repeat, the sister remains for her brother the centre of all that is sexually forbidden—its very symbol; the prototype of all unlawful sexual tendencies within the same generation and the foundation of prohibited degrees of kinship and relationship, though the taboo loses force as its application is extended. (My italics)[18]

Clearly, from these observations of Malinowski, and other anthropologists, primitive societies are mainly concerned with the regulation of the incest libido in the brother-sister relationship within the nuclear family unit. In my view, this, to us strange and complex regulation of the brother-sister relationship, contains the key to understanding the psychological meaning of incest. But first let us give some attention to mother-son and father-daughter incest.

While incest with a mother is regarded as highly reprehensible, unnatural and immoral, there is not the same feeling of horror and fear as towards brother-sister incest. When speaking with the natives about maternal incest, Malinowski found

neither the rigid suspense nor the emotional reactions which are always evoked by any allusion to brother sister relations. They would discuss the possibility without being shocked, but it was clear that they regarded incest with the mother as almost impossible. I would not affirm that such incest has never occurred, but certainly I have obtained no concrete data, and the very fact that no case survives in memory or in tradition shows that the natives take relatively little interest in it.[19]

---

18. Malinowski, *The Sexual Life of Savages*, 522.
19. *Ibid.*, 524.

In contrast to the brother-sister relationship, there is a natural sensual warmth and open communication with the mother. Of course at puberty the son is also separated from the mother. While the mother is sexually taboo, there seems to be none of the fear of expressing physical tenderness and love with her as there is with the sister. No doubt that maternal instinct and the age disparity are at work preventing excessive sexual stimulation of the young boy. Between brother and sister it is another matter, but one cannot help but wonder why such stringent measures are needed. Surely the societal attitudes toward incest become' implanted in the child's psyche at a very early age, so why must the brother-sister relationship be so unnatural? We shall return to this issue presently.

As for the father, in a matrilineal society he has no kinship relationship to his children so that sex between father and daughter is not called incest, nor is it fraught with all the terrible consequences of incest violation—fatal disease or death by other means. Nevertheless it is forbidden and regarded as reprehensible but for other reasons. One is that the father has control of his daughter's marriage and love affairs, which she discusses with him. Another is that she is his wife's nearest kinswoman. Again, "a man should not sleep with his daughter, since it was his duty to be tender to her when she was a child, to take her in his arms." So the paternal instinct would certainly seem to be at work preventing father-daughter incest. Although sexual intercourse between father and daughter does occur among the Trobrianders, it is apparently rare and viewed with definite moral repugnance.[20]

Among animals in the natural state, the parents generally force their young to fend for themselves as soon as they are old enough to do so or else they leave them. This instinctual reaction in animals tends to prevent mating between parents and children. The descriptions of family life among the Trobrianders suggest that a similar parental instinct is at work among humans preventing sex between parent and child. Of course the separation is ritualized through institutions, and

20. *The Sexual Life of Savages*, 528-31.

the break is not as total and permanent as it is with animals. On the contrary, love and respect and a permanent bond between parents and children, even if they are physically separated, is the foundation upon which the human family is built.

If the parental instincts are sufficient to prevent sexual relations between parent and child, why is there a need for an incest taboo? Perhaps such an additional precaution was needed to ensure that the parent-child intimacy would be broken, that the psychological umbilical cord would be severed when the child reached sexual maturity. There may be a more important reason for the existence of such a prohibition; a taboo always sanctifies the forbidden object. The verb *tapui* from which the word *tabu* originates, means "to make holy."[21] In this way an object is endowed with *mana* and numinosity (the awesome mystery of a divine power) and becomes a symbolic expression of an exceptional power. Without the incest taboo, children, like animals, would take parents for granted just like any other object. By sanctifying or deifying the parents, the taboo creates a psychological distance which is essential for the development of consciousness. An aura of mystery begins to surround the parents, stimulating the child's imagination to focus on the special qualities of mother and father and their relationship. Why is the child allowed such physical intimacy with them except for their sexual organs? And why does one parent have a penis and the other a vagina? Perhaps they fit together? If so, why are they allowed such intimacy and not he? Is it not dangerous for them and if not why? How is it that mother and father, who are so different in every way, seem to belong together? In other words, the taboo stimulates questions and images of the mystery of the male-female connection at an early age, and it releases the archetype of human love and sex as a sacred union. The unique human veneration of the parents is directly related to a child's early experience of the archetype of the Sacred Marriage *(hierosgamos)* in relationship to them. Parents will forever be associated with the first

---

21. G. Van Der Leeuw, *Religion in Essence and Manifestation*, Vol. I, New York: Harper Torchbooks, 1963, 44.

ROBERT STEIN

experience of the Mother and Father archetypes. Without an incest taboo toward the parents, it is doubtful that culture would have developed. But again I must emphasize that the taboo is not essential for the prevention of sexual union between parent and child.

However in the brother-sister relationship, the incest taboo is crucial in preventing sexual involvement. Still, the elaborate, stringent precautions employed by primitives cannot simply be explained on the basis of a need to prevent incest. Only in very old age, according to Mead, are brother and sister once again allowed to sit together on the same mat without shame.[22] All sociocultural attempts are inadequate to explain this complex ritualization of the brother-sister relationship. A psychological exploration of this phenomenon will, I believe, bring us closer to the heart of the incest mystery.

Until puberty the children are contained in an atmosphere of love and family unity which gives them a sense of belonging and identity which can only strengthen the bond between brother and sister. The taboo does not break this deep transpersonal connection even though it enforces physical and spiritual distance. By endowing them with an aura of mystery and numinosity, brother and sister become objects of fear and fascination, each for the other. The impossibility of personal involvement stimulates the child's interest and imagination in this fascinating look alike contemporary of the opposite sex. In all other relationships with contemporaries, the child is allowed complete sexual freedom. Therefore the main effect of the brother-sister incest taboo is to stimulate the sexual imagination in relationship to an exceptionally desirable and mysterious member of the opposite sex. Why is this so important?

Imagination is one of the basic ingredients for psychological development. Whenever an instinct is effectively inhibited from action, this stimulates the flow of internal images. While the survival instincts are primary, they cannot go unfulfilled for long. Out of all of a person's animal instincts, only the sexual instinct can endure long periods of deprivation without endangering an individual's survival. As long as a child's basic

22. Margaret Mead, *Coming of Age in Samoa*, London: Penguin, 1954, 42.

46

instinctual needs are fulfilled, the psyche remains hidden and undeveloped. Thus sexual inhibition is essential for the opening up of the imaginal world. In addition, sexual polarity is the root metaphor for creative imaginal activity: i.e., the play and tension of the opposites and their union work to form a new creation.

More than anything else the incest taboo forces an individual to become conscious of incompleteness. A boy will experience his sister as closely related to his being, yet she is an unknown "holy" other forever unattainable. He is dedicated to loving and serving her, but he can never unite with her. The same relationship applies to a girl and her brother. The longing to find and unite with the mysterious other half of oneself is a direct consequence of the brother-sister taboo. This uniquely human attribute is responsible for people's eternal fascination with all matters concerning love, sex, and the human connection. It has helped transform the sexual drive from a purely biological urge to the supreme instrument of psychological development. Above all, in longing to find a soul-mate, a person is able ultimately to discover and shape one's own soul.

Without the sexual restraint and regulation which all cultures impose, the idea of sexual union as a sacred act binding two people together permanently could not have emerged into the human imagination. This image has become part of our psychic inheritance. It appears, as we have mentioned earlier, in such archetypal forms as the heavenly marriage between King and Queen, the mystical marriage of Sun God and Moon Goddess, and the incestuous union of the Brother-Sister pair. Since all of these images of the sacred marriage, *hierosgamos,* are also representations of the soul uniting with its mate, they are *all* incestuous, and the term Incest Archetype can be conveniently used to include all such expressions.

The process of moving from childhood to adulthood involves a gradual internalization of the images of the *hierosgamos.* The incest taboo and other rituals concerned with the mysteries of sexuality are essential to this process. When a culture loses its connection to the meaning of Incest, its people suffer from an internal disharmony between the masculine/

feminine opposites. This is reflected in the disturbed relationships between the sexes and a breakdown in the vitality and stability of permanent unions—in humanity the Incest Archetype is essential for the release and maintenance of the mating instinct.

While restrictions on the spontaneous expression of sexual urges and human development appear to go hand in hand, they are also responsible for throwing humanity into a state of conflict between spiritual and animal-sensual natures. Because of this dichotomy a person is vulnerable to an infinite range of emotional pain unknown to other creatures—this is the psychological significance contained in the myth of the Fall. On the other hand, humans are also gifted with an imagination which makes it possible for them to reconcile these opposites; to experience the untold joy of finding new and better ways to return to Paradise.

The limitations society has imposed upon sexual instinct make it impossible for us to be completely free sensually and bodily in relationship to others. Yet in the ever-expanding world of the imagination which this opens, spirit has unlimited freedom. There is nothing to prevent the imagination from doing anything or going any place one desires. One is free to transgress any sexual taboo and reconcile the conflict between mind and body. One can return again and again to an original paradisiacal state of wholeness, before one's spiritual and animal natures are separated. The joys that open to an imaginal world more than compensate for the limitations imposed upon us by the mundane world. In addition imagination gives us the possibility of effecting changes in the mundane world, of creating new possibilities for sharing our joys with others.

CHAPTER FOUR

The Incest Wound

T here has been a deterioration of the social forms which enable parent, child, and siblings to experience instinctual sexuality without guilt and fear of violating the incest taboo. This has destroyed the intimate and essential kinship connection between mother and son, father and daughter, brother and sister, individual and community. The awareness of the fundamental importance of the incest taboo for psychic development and wholeness has been lost. Consequently, the incest taboo instead of being dealt with consciously has fallen into the unconscious and functions autonomously. This means that the necessity for taking precautions against incest, or the danger of violating the incest taboo, is no longer a conscious problem. When the sexual instinct then threatens to break through the incest barrier, sexuality is experienced as something dangerous and sinful. In this way the moral conflict, which rightfully belongs to the mystery of incest, becomes focused on instinctual sexuality. Instead of fearing incest, we fear sexuality as well as our instincts in general.

The elaborate precautions taken by "primitives" to prevent a violation of the incest taboo suggest that the intensity of the incest desire is too strong to be left to individual responsibility. In fact, much of the social and religious structure of primitive societies is related to the incest taboo.[1] In contrast, our modern Western civilization lacks viable rituals and social forms for regulating the

---

1. See the works cited of Layard, Malinowski, and Crawly.

49

incest libido. Thus the responsibility for preventing incest, for dealing with the whole mystery of incest, has come to rest largely on the individual.

Although there are indications that the incest taboo has become as powerful in the human psyche as the incest desire, it takes a high degree of ego consciousness for an *individual* to withstand the fatal touch of incest without being split by the heat of the emotions released. The growing child has always been protected from too much exposure to the fascinating temptation of incest. But now little is left of these protective and integrating rituals, and the child is forced to solve alone the moral conflict involving the deepest mysteries of life. Most of the time this results in a repression of sexuality, but it is not uncommon, when there is open sexual provocation by the adult, that the child is unable to repress the sexuality. In these cases the spiritual feelings of warmth and tenderness are repressed. For example, a woman patient with a negative father complex could remember no instances where she felt love or closeness to her father. Her only pleasant memories of him were primarily related to sexuality; i.e., actual sexual contact as well as fantasies. In another instance, a man remembers, without the slightest guilt, having had strong sexual desires and fantasies toward his mother; he too could remember no close or warm moments with her. These examples illustrate that the incest wound causes a split between Eros[2] and sexuality. They also call attention to the fact that it is not the repression of sexuality which is crucial but the problem of incest.

Since the taboo is so essential for the humanization and cultural development of people, it is understandable that its violation should evoke such guilt and fear. A "primitive" would have to be insane and totally overwhelmed by an uncontrollable desire, in order to risk the consequences of committing incest. As long as there was a thread of rational control left, a "primitive" would

---

2. Following in the Platonic tradition, Eros will be used to refer to the full range of human love and passion—psychic and erotic, and not in the Freudian sense as undifferentiated sexual energies or libido.

resist desire. This is essentially what a child in our culture must do: repress any spontaneous incestuous sexual impulses. Actually the "primitive" is far better off because that society's social forms protect from too much stimulation of incestuous tendencies. By the time "primitives" reach puberty, their sexuality has transformed sufficiently so that they need not fear losing rational control or violating the incest taboo if they react spontaneously and instinctually.

For a child in our Western culture, quite the opposite is true. As long as one was sexually immature generally, one had little difficulty controlling and repressing forbidden sexual urges. But with puberty all repressed sexual urges and fantasies return in full force. This is when one experiences the first real horror about incestuous desires. One attempts to deal with this guilt and fear by exercising constant control over what enters consciousness. Depending on the severity of the incest wound, a person may be forced to repress all sexual imagery in order to be sure that none of the guilt-provoking fantasies invade the psyche. Fortunately most children do not have to use such extreme measures, but when they do, it results in almost a total cut off from the sexual instinct. Such children have a tendency to panic at the slightest sign of losing rational control.

In the more typical Western pattern, only nonincestuous sexuality is allowed to enter the consciousness; this means that feelings of kinship connection and all the romantic, loving fantasies of spiritual intimacy are prevented from entering consciousness along with sexual imagery. This internal split between love and sex, the spiritual and animal portions of the soul, is a direct consequence of the incest wound. When the tension between the incest desire and prohibition is obliterated, fragmentation results and the essential internal union between the feminine/masculine opposites is not possible.

Most people have difficulty connecting emotionally with this comprehension although they may appreciate its logic. It rings a bell only for those who were unsuccessful or only partially successful in repressing their incestuous sexuality. It is not really essential that one

51

dig up repressed incestuous fantasies and experiences, as long as one becomes aware of how the mind/body, love/sex split manifests itself in everyday life.

I believe the severity of the wound can be measured by the degree of fear one has of losing rational control, whether or not it is directly related to sexuality. Those who experience the pain of frequent rejection in relationships are probably also severely wounded. So too are those who are frequently thrown into a state of confusion, loss of identity, and emotional paralysis in their intimate relationships. Of course, the most obvious manifestation of the wound occurs when sexuality becomes obstructed in all ways except in relation to fantasies or to an actual person for whom one feels neither love nor respect. Why is there such horror of losing rational control, of allowing irrational and spontaneous emotions or desires to express themselves without ego censor? Is it because a person fears going amok and committing horrible crimes? Most people have little more to fear than making fools of themselves or, at worst, committing some offensive but forgivable aggressive act. Then why is there such an overwhelming fear of being totally wiped out if one should let go of the reins on the instincts? Surely this has more to do with fantasy, with inner reality, than with the actual dangers confronting a person from outer reality. What, then, is going on inside when one is caught in this ego trap?

I remember a shocking dream I had when I first became aware of the depth of my own incest wound: It was about 11 P.M. and I had to go to my office for something. As I opened the door I suddenly became frightened, sensing some ominous presence in the room. I switched on the light, but saw no one. Suddenly I heard a noise like a whimper coming from behind me. I turned to discover a small, ragged twelve year old boy crouching under my desk. I awakened, terrified. Later, using the technique of active imagination which Jung suggests, I reentered the dream in fantasy. And this is what happened: I pulled the frightened boy out from under my desk and demanded to know what he was doing there. At first he refused to answer, but finally he told me he hides under my desk all the time when I see patients. Then turning to me with a lustful grin he said, "I really dig all those sexy stories your patients tell you."

I became furious, calling him a sex maniac, and threatened to turn him over to the police. Then he broke down and my heart went out to him. I took him into my arms. Between sobs he told me how I had abandoned him when I was twelve because of my guilt about my own sexuality and that I have forced him to go underground out of fear of my own lust. There was more to the fantasy, but this is the heart of it. Obviously this little boy was symbolic of that animal-sensual part of myself which I had repressed. It was at about the age of twelve that I began having strong sexual desires toward my sisters. I suspect I must have felt the same terrible dread of incest which a primitive feels. One can imagine how fearful I must have been, at the time of this dream, of losing rational control if all my repressed incestuous sexuality lurked just under the protective front of the physician's desk.

A young woman dreams of having an hour with her analyst when suddenly the door begins to open. She is shocked and furious when she sees who it is, and she quickly rushes to the door and pushes the young teenage girl out of the room. Who was it? Only a girl she had known in high school who was cheap and had the bad reputation of being an easy lay. The dream is obvious–she feared letting her own immoral, lustful sensual side enter into the analytical relationship. Since the analyst invariably constellates a parental archetype, one may assume the incestuous origins of her fear. In fact, until this dream revealed the nature of her fear, she had been extremely defensive and resistant to the analytical process.

Such examples of the soul-splitting effects of repressed incestuous sexuality are plentiful and relatively easy to grasp once they have been revealed. However there are many other expressions of the incest wound which are not so obvious. For example, sexual desire may not become fully aroused except in a triangular situation. As soon as the triangle is broken so, too, does the desire diminish. This may seem contradictory because one would expect that the incest fear would inhibit sexuality in a triangular situation. We shall have to look deeper into the nature of the wound in order to understand this paradox.

Recall that when children are excessively provoked, they may be unable to repress their sexuality so they are forced to repress their feelings of love and kinship. We must not forget that the purpose of the incest taboo is to prevent children from having sexual union in those relationships where they feel the greatest spiritual intimacy. Thus incest guilt can be avoided so long as one is unaware of experiencing one of these opposites—love or sex. The repressed opposite will, however, continually threaten to enter consciousness because of the soul's fundamental need for union. In other words, the longing for incestuous union, even though it is repressed, is as powerful as is our horror of violating the taboo. The more we repress it, the more power it gains over us, so that we are continually fascinated by and falling into incestuous types of involvements. So long as we remain unconscious of the repressed other half, we do not experience the guilt and painful conflict. Innocently we plunge from one relationship to another, emerging each time fragmented and disillusioned.

I think of a severe, but typical, example of a person who was unable to allow the repressed opposite to enter consciousness. This woman was continually fascinated by men who had authority, position, superior intellect, or special talents. She always felt inadequate and incapable of experiencing sexual passion with them. In the few instances in which she did attempt involvement, she felt as if her soul and body were raped, and she ended up wounded and furious. This woman had great love and respect for her father until puberty when he had made several sexual advances toward her. In analysis she talked at first only of her good feelings toward him because she had blocked out the sexual episodes. When they were finally brought back into consciousness, all the fury returned which she had experienced at the age of thirteen. She felt that her father was an impotent, dirty old man who had her trusting youthful innocence. From some of the details which she related of her relationship to her father, it was obvious she

54

was not all that innocent. But she was unable emotionally to accept her own sexual involvement with him. Consequently the pattern continued to repeat itself in relationship to men whom she admired. Her feeling of inadequacy was due to the fact that she was unable to bring her natural, instinctive self into these relationships—how could she if she feared and rejected her sexuality?

But there was another side to this. She also found herself compulsively fascinated by irresponsible, intellectually inferior, psychopathic men. With them her sexual passion was released, and to that extent the relationships were much more gratifying. But as she was unable to allow herself to love such men, she experienced great pain because of the lack of spiritual communion. In addition, she tended to fall into a sexual bondage with them, which paralyzed her free will and undermined her self respect. If she had been able to allow herself to experience consciously her love and kinship feeling toward these men, she would have become free instead of imprisoned and fragmented.

Another common manifestation of the incest wound is the experience of loving someone sexually and spiritually in fantasy but being cut off or unable to express such feelings in actuality. This situation often comes from the fear of consciously embracing the phallic or aggressive aspects of the sexual instinct. The incestuous guilt associated with aggressive sexuality prevents such people from initiating the flow of eros, although they may be very responsive to the initiating action of others. In this way they can remain unconscious of their aggressive impulses and therefore feel innocent.

Still another important, but more complex, manifestation of the wound can be illustrated as follows: A woman, caught in a psychological marriage to her father, had repressed her unfulfilled incestuous longings to actually marry him. She hated her father and felt betrayed by him, but she did not know why. Her relationships with men were generally short-lived, ending abruptly, and painfully. She was always threatened by spiritual intimacy with a man but open to sexual intimacy. Typically, as soon as she would become sexually involved, she was inundated with all her repressed incestuous longings, except that her current lover took the place of her father. In her fantasies, her lover-father would declare his undying love, sweep her off her feet, and carry her to the church where they would be married to live happily ever after. These romantic fantasies were so powerful that to her they became a *fait accompli.* Invariably, the actual man had no such feelings, and she was rudely shaken out of her dreams, but always with the conviction that she had been deeply wounded and deceived by the man. It had all been so real for her that she never knew if she had imagined it or if the man had really said such things and led her on. Whenever this happened she was left paralyzed, confused, and humiliated for weeks and sometimes months. Essentially, the effect of the incest wound on this woman was to make it difficult for her to differentiate between inner and outer reality in her relationships. To a lesser or greater extent, this difficulty is an inevitable effect of the wound.

As long as the desire for incestuous union remains unconscious, it will be activated in every relationship which offers the possibility of soul connection. This has the effect of obstructing the natural, spontaneous flow of love because the Incest archetype always demands eternal commitment in a sacred marriage. Simply put, if I feel compelled to make a permanent commitment every time love moves me toward union with another, will this not make me cautious and fearful of loving? One must be free to love or not love, to feel and express love in the quick of the moment whether or not it lasts forever. The incest wound interferes with this freedom because of the soul's longing for the sacred eternal union with its mate. This needs to be experienced as an inner reality and not as an outer demand whenever one feels love for another.

Apart from love and sex, the incest wound tends to interfere with the experience and spontaneous expression of all the aggressive instincts. In part this comes from the same fear of losing rational control, but it is also a direct consequence of the guilt-evoking incestuous triangle. A son will fear standing up to his father, which reveals his own aggressive potency because of his guilt about his unconscious incestuous marriage to his mother. The same conflict applies to a woman in relationship to her mother. The more severe the wound the more the child experiences the inner parent as rejecting of his or her nature. This may ultimately lead to an obsessive need to gain approval and acceptance from others.

The primary function of the incest prohibition is to bring the untamed instincts into the service of love and kinship through a process which stimulates the formation of images of the male-female union. This is not the same as the *repression* of instincts which seems so necessary in our modern civilization. When the repression of instincts becomes necessary in a culture, it is a sign that something has gone wrong with the societal institutions for the regulation of incest.

CHAPTER FIVE

Infantile Sexuality and Narcissism

Infantile sexuality, like everything infantile, is characterized by its compulsive, demanding quality, and its total lack of concern for the needs of others. As a consequence of the incest wound, there is often a severe repression of the still immature sexual instinct. The obstructed instinct then invades and contaminates every aspect of the child's personality, and almost every attempt at spontaneous expression, from the highest to the lowest, will have a demanding, destructive, and regressive infantile aspect to it. The first step in healing such childhood wounds is the full exploration and acceptance of every aspect of one's sexual life, in both its concrete and imaginal expressions. I suspect Henry Miller was involved in such a process when he wrote his famous *Tropic* books, particularly when he says something to the effect that the surest way of transforming the worst in oneself is to accept it fully and joyfully. Although the sexuality Miller describes is usually associated with masculine psychology, women suffer as much from their own unrelated and undeveloped sexuality as do men.

But acceptance alone is insufficient. The experience of the transforming effects of love is also essential. For example, obsessive infantile and sadomasochistic fantasies practically disappear during the acute phase of being in love, and sexuality enters into the service of Eros. This remarkable fact is understandable since the feelings of dedication and service to another which love evokes are incompatible with infantilism.

The term narcissistic is generally used psychologically to refer to an individual preoccupied with love of self and having difficulty establishing a love relationship with another person. However, we tend to place people in this category who are as incapable of self love as they are of loving another. While they may be obsessively trying to satisfy their own needs and have little or no concern about the needs of others, this does not mean they love themselves. On the contrary, the so-called narcissistic individual has an insatiable need to be loved, which comes from a loathing and rejection of vital parts of oneself rather than self-love.

Underlying a pathological preoccupation with oneself is the need for self-expression. Certainly this is true of the child's natural absorption with its needs and thoughts. However in the adult the lack of any concern or interest in the needs of others would point to a fixation at a childhood state of development. The family and culture soon enough make the child aware that it must give consideration to the needs of others, that it must come to some balance between the subjective needs of its own nature and the needs which the objects in its environment seem to have.

Giving is an outgoing act and taking is a receptive act. An excellent symbol for the outgoing, for that which fills and pours out, is Phallos; and Womb is perhaps the symbol, *par excellence*, for the vessel which receives, contains, protects, and nourishes. A human connection is soon broken if the flow is only in one direction. The person who is functioning as the container can only hold so much and then the flow must be reversed or a dam, some form of resistance, will necessarily intervene to break the connection. The circulation of Eros between two individuals is dependent on a reciprocal relationship between input and output.

The phenomenon of falling in love, when it is mutual, is perhaps a special instance in which there is a reciprocal acceptance and perfect response of each person to the needs of the other. Sensitivity becomes remarkably acute among lovers. If we accept the state of being in love as a model for a harmonious type of human relationship, we can use it as a basis of comparison with other kinds of relationships. At the opposite pole, we find the type of relationship usually experienced by the individual preoccupied only with selfish needs. (Before continuing it might be worthwhile to consider the individual who is primarily concerned with the needs of others. Culturally and socially this would appear to be a more mature state of development. However it does not necessarily lead to better or closer human relationships: the flow is still in one direction and this eventually leads to stasis).

Returning now to the state of being "in love," let us examine this remarkable phenomenon more closely. It is, first of all, a highly personal experience in which one's whole being becomes primarily focused on the loved object. At the same time, there is an acute awakening of all senses. Ortega y Gasset sees this exclusiveness of attention as a paralysis of consciousness. "Attention," he says, "is the supreme instrument of personality; it is the apparatus which regulates our mental lives. When paralysed, it does not leave us any freedom of movement. In order to save ourselves, we would have to reopen the field of consciousness, and to achieve that it would be necessary to introduce other objects into its focus to rupture the beloved's exclusiveness." . . ."We have been entrapped in an hermetic enclosure that has no opening to the outside world. Nothing from the outside is able to penetrate and facilitate our escape. The soul of a man in love smells of the closed up room of a sick man—its confined atmosphere is filled with stale breath."[1] Obviously he sees the concentration of consciousness on the loved object and the hermetic enclosure which contains lovers as a negative process. This attitude reflects the typical masculine prejudice against Eros which forms selective attachments, as opposed to the spirit which soars unattached and free. For Ortega, "The more masculine one is, in a spiritual sense, the more the mind is disjointed in separate compartments."[2] No wonder he sees the state of being in love as a paralysis of consciousness and as an imprisonment of the soul! Eros, of all life's forces, has the power to break down these separate chambers of the mind and to heal the mind/body dichotomy. The unifying experience of being in love enlarges consciousness: through the intense connection which one has with the loved object, one embraces and enters into relationship with the cosmos.

---

1. Ortega y Gasset, *On Love*, New York: Meridian Books, 1960, 52.
2. *Ibid.*, 74.

The separate compartments which the masculine principle seems to value so highly is the real source of stagnation which produces the foul smell of the sick room. However we look at it, Eros, the principle of psychic relatedness, is the key to spiritual freedom. It is the key which unlocks all doors thus releasing the imprisoned spirit so that it may enter into the circulating stream of the micro- and macro-cosmos. In this way it initiates a process of purification, distillation, and transformation—the true basis for renewal and creative living. Eros is the great opener, penetrating the most solidly sealed compartments.

The feminine principle (womb) functions primarily to nourish, protect, and contain; the masculine principle (phallos) seeks the fertile container of the feminine so that it may give full expression to its own uniqueness in form and substance. Since we are not speaking about male or female, but about principles, both factors are at work in either sex. Behind the infantilism of the ego-centered, self-occupied, over-demanding individual, is the restless and disgruntled spirit seeking desperately for an adequate container. Such individuals have no possibility of overcoming their "narcissism" or "infantilism" short of finding an adequate container. But the problem is internal as well as external; finding a creative expression or someone who is truly understanding and accepting is, therefore, an inadequate solution. Psychological transformation is dependent on the intermingling and circulation of the soul; it is not enough that the soul or spirit is able to pour out, it must be able to reenter, and for this the individual needs to become Womb as well as Phallos. For a man this means getting in touch with the feminine principle, the anima.[3] The demanding, self-centered woman is usually under the power of the negative animus,[4] so that she, too, needs to reconnect with her own basic feminine nature.

Falling in love is one sure way of opening the circuits. Even the most emotionally infantile individuals transform and suddenly become more concerned about their loved one than about themselves. This

---

3. Anima is Jung's term for the feminine components of a man's psyche.
4. The animus is the term Jung has coined for the phallic or masculine aspects of a woman's nature.

genuine love and concern for the welfare of another is a function of Eros. No amount of analysis or understanding of oneself will effect a transformation of the psyche unless the old wound is opened by the arrow of Eros, and a union of the masculine and feminine opposites occurs on all levels throughout the circulating stream of life.

In this age of isolation and fragmentation, we long desperately for the healing which only Eros can bring, yet we are filled with fear and trembling whenever we are in its presence. We seek all possible substitutes, from the sacred to the most profane. In spite of this we are not immune to the son of Aphrodite. And when Eros does succeed in its task, it is as if the accumulated waters of a thousand centuries has suddenly been unleashed, and the violence of our reactions is indicative of the terrible hunger we have suffered. Only when thus stricken, do we lose our fear of Eros. It soon returns, however, when the magic begins to wane.

Why this fear of Eros? When Eros appears as the "mighty daimon," it is indeed a force to be feared. Perhaps it so frequently takes this threatening form in our Western world because it must break through the armor of compartmentalized thinking. On the other hand, it takes the powerful thrust of a daimonic force to move people out of their biological tendency toward inertia. The powerful emotion which moves people toward union can, indeed, destroy as well as renew. A creative conscious connection to Eros is, therefore, essential, but we must delay further discussion of this fundamental issue until Part Four.

CHAPTER SIX

The Archetypal Family Situation

The experience of the archetypal Mother and Father in relationship to the personal parents is essential for the psychological development of the child. If this fundamental experience is disrupted too early in life, it seriously effects ego development. On the other hand, the emergence of the ego from the unconscious is dependent on the gradual withdrawal of the archetypal projections which the parents have incarnated. The initial withdrawal of these projections probably occurs through a process of transference or displacement. That is, the grandparents, a close relative, a teacher, or even a movie star will begin to carry some of the archetype, and the parents then begin to assume more human proportions. In a matriarchal culture, as we have seen, the mother's brother assumes more and more of the role of the archetypal father while the relationship with the actual father becomes more equal and personal as the child develops.[1] This loosening of the archetypal projections from the true parents also initiates a movement toward internalization of the father and mother archetypes. Several things then go hand in hand: the withdrawal of the projections primarily through transference but accompanied also by some internalization, plus the beginning of a more personal, human, and equal relationship with the actual parents. If the archetypal projections are not eventually withdrawn from the parents, the individual tends to fall into the role of either the archetypal child or parent in all relationships; this makes it extremely difficult for a child to experience

---

1. Malinowski, *Sexual Life of Savages.*

an equal and individualized relationship with anyone. This is one of the most serious consequences of what psychologists call a mother or father fixation.

Just how important is it that a more personal, less archetypal relationship should be experienced with the actual parents? If the parents refuse to relinquish their archetypal roles: the child's relationship with them becomes difficult and unpleasant, to say the least. What possible effects must this have on the child? Surely, the child must wonder if the price paid for individuality is worth it, if it would not be better off to remain in the more secure and pleasurable archetypal child role. And, of course, if the parents refuse to move toward a more human and personal level with the child, it makes it much more difficult for the child to withdraw the projections. Under such conditions a child can only accomplish the withdrawal by cutting off all emotional ties to the parents—which is not only painful but a destructive loss of an essential bond. This far-too-common resolution of the archetypal parent-child relationship makes the individual extremely fearful of and reluctant to enter into deep emotional relationships in the future.

With these considerations in mind, there should be little doubt that a positive, more individual relationship to the parents is extremely important for the development of an integrated personality. In analysis, the archetypal parent-child situation is reactivated. Central to a healing analytical relationship is the experience of a nonwounding transition from the archetypal to a more personal connection between analysand and analyst.

Every new human encounter demands an act of faith—trust that the other will do one no harm, that the intentions are honorable and benevolent—if the relationship is to continue and develop. Since we cannot possibly know the dark and intricate movements of another human being's soul in our initial meetings, an affirmative response depends primarily on the constellation of positive archetypal forces.

THE ARCHETYPAL FAMILY SITUATION

Many individuals consistently react with distrust and suspicion. In some cases this negative response is only in relationship to members of the opposite sex, but in others it may be to members of the same sex. Some severely disturbed people seem unable to experience an initial positive feeling to either sex. It is especially revealing to examine the dreams of individuals who consistently react negatively to members of the same, opposite, or both sexes. A long series of dreams will painfully demonstrate an almost total lack of any positive and benevolent masculine or feminine images, as the case may be. On the contrary, the appearance of negative, threatening, and usually highly charged masculine or feminine imagery will be the most frequent motif in the dramatic structure of the dream.

I have elsewhere written about a schizophrenic young woman which had a tragic ending.[2] Not only did she have great fear and distrust of men and of the world, but she had an almost equally negative reaction to women. Her isolation was, of course, severe except for a thin and tenuous connection with another woman. A dream series extending over a period of approximately six months was almost totally lacking in any positive masculine or feminine figures. On the few occasions in which apparently positive images did appear, they would change into sinister figures by the end of the dream. This woman had an extremely negative relationship to her mother, a hostile and bitter woman. Her father had abandoned her mother before she was born, and she had memories only of her mother's resentment and vindictiveness toward him and towards men. Without going into further detail, this case illustrates the correlation between a deficiency or lack of positive archetypal masculine and feminine image formation in the unconscious, and the extremely negative, paranoid reaction of the patient to both men and women. In this instance at least, it would appear that the traumatic nature of the parent-child relationship was largely responsible for her inability to experience the protective and benevolent aspects of the Father and Mother archetypes.

---

2. Robert Stein, *Analytical Psychology and Healing*, Zürich, unpublished dissertation, 1959.

Let us assume that every child is potentially able to have this fundamental archetypal experience, given the necessary external stimulus, although this may not be true in certain types of psychopathology where there may be an inherent structural archetypal defect.[3] Excluding this possibility, it is improbable that a child would not have had the experience of the positive parental archetypes.

The splitting of the archetype into positive and negative components belongs to the process of the withdrawal of archetypal projections, the development of the ego consciousness, and the growing recognition on the part of the child of its own individual personality. In relationship to the parents or parent substitutes, this means moving from the archetypal toward a more personal relationship. In this movement an aspect of the archetype can be so badly fragmented that it loses all form and substance.[4] This makes it impossible for the gradual process of internalization to occur, unless the archetype is first reformed through another experience. When this happens the movement from the wholeness of the original archetypal situation to the incompleteness of the more personal relationship, even when there is a relatively smooth transition, is always accompanied by an experience of pain and loss. When the harsh outline of merely human proportions begins to emerge from the soft and enveloping archetypal mist, one always experiences a sense of disillusionment. But simultaneously one gains a new sense of freedom and strength. In the case of a child, whether or not a gain is also experienced depends largely on the attitude of the parent, plus the forms and rituals which should help to regulate a smooth rite of passage in every culture. Where the rite of passage is unsuccessful, a huge rent occurs in the ego-soul axis. The child is then forced to protect this gaping wound by putting up a wall against any close human connection. However, the child may have less fear of opening up to men than to women, or vice versa, depending on some of the factors we discussed above. The whole

---

3. Stein, unpublished dissertation, 97.
4. Contrast this view with Fordham's deintegration of Self theory. Michael Fordham, *New Developments in Analytical Psychology*, London: Routledge, 1957.

experience leaves the child with a feeling of having been stabbed in the back, betrayed by the person who was most loved and trusted. We all know how deep the pain of betrayal goes in adulthood; it is even deeper and more devastating to a child.

REJECTION AND BETRAYAL

Let us study more closely the mechanisms that are usually set into motion where one has been deeply wounded through a childhood experience of betrayal and disillusionment. The child experiences rejection and betrayal when the transition, from the wholeness of the original archetypal situation to the more human personal relationship is missing or inadequate. This occurs, for example, when a mother continues to identify with the archetypal all-protective, as-nourishing Mother role even though other, quite opposite feelings and emotions are coming into her relationship with her child. The child needs to experience a more total picture of her true personality so that the child, too, can begin to experience more individuality.

When the mother identifies with the positive Mother archetype, the negative Mother will be strongly constellated in her unconscious. The child, instead of experiencing a transition from the archetypal Mother to the more human mother, with many shadings of feelings and emotions, is caught between two opposing archetypal forces. This abruptly destroys the child's sense of wholeness, producing a large rent in personality, and this experience is one of rejection and betrayal. The child resents being thrust out of the containment of the positive mother-child archetypal situation, but at the same time this impulse toward individuation urges the child to move on. The child's choices are limited: either to remain a child or to evoke the wrath of the *absolute* rejecting and demanding Negative Mother. There is nothing in between. The child is therefore faced with a dark power which destroys any sense of gratification or accomplishment even if moved towards the goal of giving form and expression to individuality. This is how the child has been betrayed.

69

To the same degree that the Positive Mother accepts and cherishes the child's nature with all its weaknesses and inadequacies, the Negative Mother rejects it and demands that its insufficiencies be overcome. This occurs on a very collective level, however, so that it amounts to a rejection of all that is unique and individual in the child; or all the factors that do not live up to an image the mother may have of how her child should be. The consequence of such an experience is that the child must hide or repress its own uniqueness, and these qualities become incorporated into the shadow.[5] Since the shadow always contains many things which are really unacceptable, repugnant, and destructive to others and to society, such contamination of individuality and shadow can be disastrous. The individual then experiences acceptance of the soul and shadow as identical. This makes it extremely difficult for a person to establish or maintain a close human connection with anyone. Whenever one begins to get close to such a person, that person will invariably do something to be rejected. We need to try to understand more about this phenomenon since it is so common.

Why does someone suffering from the deep archetypal wound of betrayal seem to continually provoke rejection? It is almost as if something in the person is asking for rejection. Such an individual often expresses just this view about themselves. For some time I thought this was entirely owing to a fear of closeness, which exposes the old wound to further injury. This certainly made sense until I realized that although the wound may be exposed in the openness of a close human connection, it is the childhood experience of betrayal and rejection which caused the wound in the first place. Therefore, when a person both rejects and provokes rejection, the original wounding situation is repeated. Obviously the person does not avoid suffering through these unconscious mechanisms. Let us look for other explanations.

---

5. The term shadow refers to all those rejected and repressed aspects of the personality; it contains infantile, inferior, and morally reprehensible tendencies, but it is also the carrier of many rejected natural, life-promoting impulses.

THE ARCHETYPAL FAMILY SITUATION

The facts are better understood if they are seen as a consequence of a person's inability to distinguish between shadow and soul. This evokes deep feelings of shame, guilt, and fear whenever such an individual enters into a communion with another soul. In other words, there are infantile and regressive elements in the shadow which should have been assimilated and integrated into the personality, but this has not happened because of the experience of severe rejection by the internalized negative parental archetype. Therefore whenever such a soul-shadow contamination exists, the individual still feels rejected even though there is acceptance and love for the person. This person demands that the other individual redeem them from the guilt they feel about the truly *unacceptable* and *destructive* aspects of their shadow, which they have not differentiated from the totality of their being. Shadow elements such as infantile demands and dependency needs, infantile or undifferentiated sexuality, greed, brutality, etc., though they belong to the human condition, must be generally contained, or they do injury to others. Acceptance of these qualities in another goes along with the love and respect one person has for another's soul, but it does not mean that one is willing to be victimized by the shadow. But this is precisely what is sought by those individuals who provoke rejection. That is, that they should be allowed to give full expression to their shadow, and that they should be loved for the punishment which it inflicts—they feel that only then will they experience true acceptance and love. This throws a somewhat different light on the problem and points to a need to get closer rather than to a fear of being close. To put it another way, there is a need to rid oneself of the guilt and fear-provoking elements of the shadow, which is why it is continually being brought into those relationships which offer the possibility of a close human connection.

REJECTION AND RESISTANCE IN ANALYSIS

A positive transference[6] reactivates the primary archetypal situation and the experience of wholeness, but this also evokes the fear of closeness, when the individual has been wounded in childhood by an unsatisfactory transition from the archetypal to a more human personal relationship with the parents. This results in a splitting of the archetype, and the parent or parents are experienced as the *Absolute Good* or *Absolute Bad* parent with none of the more human shadings in between. Individuals who have been wounded in this way experience an unconscious guilt and fear whenever they become involved in a positive relationship. They fear that the opposite demanding and rejecting archetypal force will soon take over to destroy the sense of dignity and wholeness they have realized in the closeness of a human connection. This fear eventually provokes a repetition of the childhood trauma. The destructive pattern will continue until the original wound is healed.

One of the most healing experiences in analysis occurs when the patient can experience the movement from the containment of the positive transference to a more mature and equal human relationship with the analyst. This can occur only if the negative archetypal mother or father does not remain projected onto the analyst for too long. Since the analyst is always affected by archetypal projections, it is inevitable that the analyst will often react in a way identical to the demanding and rejecting archetypal Mother or Father. Whether or not the analyst reveals a reaction is beside the point; the patient still experiences the analyst as the incarnation of the negative archetype, and rightly so. Therefore the analyst must become conscious of where one is caught as soon as possible. But this alone is not sufficient, because the nature of the doctor-patient relationship makes it difficult to establish a more equal and personal connection. Consequently, if the analyst is able to

6. The term transference is used in psychoanalysis to refer to the patient's transfer of a repressed experience from therapist onto the analyst; in archetypal psychology it refers to the mutual archetypal projections between analyst and analysand. These differences will be clarified in chapter 13.

be disentangled from the negative archetype, the relationship usually slips back into the positive archetypal situation. Still no transition occurs to a more human level. What can the analyst do to promote this transition? Simply put, the analyst must overcome the fear of hurting the patient and the fear of destroying the positive archetypal connection. This means the analyst has to be able to reveal negative affects. If patients are confronted with the way in which they effect the analyst as a human being, not as a doctor, this helps bring them into contact with the doctor as a total personality, not an archetype. Even though patients may feel hurt and rejected by what is said, they become aware that they are involved with another human soul, who has very human emotions and reactions; each time this occurs it helps to heal the split in the ego-soul axis.

THE DUAL PARENT MYTH

What is behind the myth of the child with two sets of parents? Why does this idea appear so frequently in the fantasies of children? This phenomenon is directly related to the process of detaching the archetypal image from the actual parents. As children gradually experience a humanization of their parents, the archetypal image of the Royal Couple is both transferred and internalized. At this stage of development children often feel that their actual parents are not their true parents. The fantasy follows a fairly typical form: My true parents are very rich and famous, a king and queen, and I am really a prince (or princess). The movement reflected in this fantasy will create feelings of separation anxiety and insecurity in the child, but it is also the beginning of a sense of individuality and independence from the actual parents. When a culture lacks viable rituals and containers to nurture this process, the lack promotes inner disharmony between the masculine and feminine principles, between spirit and matter, reason and feeling. Even rare children who are fortunate enough to experience a vital and harmonious connection between their parents need the help of the community, or they, too, will be fragmented in their passage into manhood or womanhood.

Unfortunately most of the viable rituals of transition have deteriorated in the West, especially in America. This breakdown has its origins in the Greek and Judeo-Christian roots of the Western psyche, which has lived with the myth that consciousness frees humanity's will to go against nature, *contra naturum*. This has resulted in the severe mind/body dichotomy which now threatens to destroy consciousness, for it seems that the split can only be healed by the obliteration of consciousness. The movement in this direction is frightening; there is a compulsive desperation in the way the hordes seek for healing, wholeness, and release from the painful agony of the mind/body split by attempting to drown themselves in passion, violence, sensual pleasure, drugs, alcohol, etc. Nature will have its revenge. To go against Nature, to reject it, is like rejecting the mother, and though consciousness can function in this way, the price is fragmentation and alienation.

The Western attitude that the development of consciousness is *contra naturum* would seem to be in need of some reevaluation. If we see consciousness as arising out of a transformation of Nature, and the further development of consciousness as a process in which humanity uses consciousness to enter into a harmonious participation with Nature (a much more Eastern view), then the separation between mind and body becomes unnecessary. Still the Western way cannot simply be thrown out as a horrendous error.

The development of the individual ego certainly involves a process of restricting and taming one's own nature, so it follows that the development of civilization may well have necessitated this differentiation and separation between the spiritual and animal natures of humans. But once the horse has been tamed and bridled, it is destructive to try forcefully and brutally to gain complete mastery over it. The relationship between human and horse must become harmonious and loving; the true Master is so in tune with the horse that a bridle is not necessary. Simply put, Western humanity has not been willing to relinquish any of the power gained in conquering Nature. Out of fear of losing power, the West continues to abuse and neglect its horse. The difficulty is that the power of consciousness lies in individuality, while Mother Nature cherishes all of her children equally and indiscriminately. Thus modern people˙ regard the giving up or giving back of any power to Nature as a loss of individuality. Furthermore, the repressive measures which people have taken against Nature has resulted in a tremendous building up of dark and violent powers in their own souls which threaten to erupt at any moment.

Then how can people reestablish a harmonious relationship with Nature and become whole again, without a total loss of thousands of centuries of hard-earned consciousness? We cannot afford to submit to the Wotanic power and frenzy of another Hitler as did the German people. The rational mind must yield up some of its power, but how can this be done without losing the tenuous foothold on reason which we still have? Depth psychotherapy has thrown much light on the individual solution. But an individual solution can at best be only relatively successful if there are not corresponding cultural changes. Using the insights which analytical psychology has given us, we can perhaps find a historical link which will open the door to a collective as well as individual solution. I think the myth of Oedipus is such a link which reveals the nature and origins of the Western mind/body split and also points toward its ultimate resolution.

CHAPTER SEVEN

The Oedipus Myth and the Incest Archetype

O edipus Rex: Synopsis of *Oedipus the King* by Sophocles.

The King and Queen of Thebes, Laius and Jocasta, are informed by an oracle that if they have a son, this son will kill his father and marry his mother. When Jocasta does give birth to a son, Oedipus, they decide to escape their fate by killing him. The infant is given to a shepherd who is to abandon him on a lonely mountain. But the Theban herdsman hands him over to a man from Corinth who presents the infant to Polybus, the childless King of Corinth. The King and Queen of Corinth adopt Oedipus and bring him up as their own son. When Oedipus becomes a young man, a drunken guest at a banquet reproaches him with not being the King's son. Though his foster-parents repudiate the slander, the young prince is not satisfied and secretly sets forth to ask the Oracle at Delphi. The Oracle does not answer his question but threatens him with the awful doom of becoming his mother's husband and his father's murderer. In order to avoid his fate, he vows to leave his parents forever. Not daring to return to Corinth, he leaves Delphi by another route, through Phokis, passing a narrow cross road. Here he is to meet his real father. When the King's herald cries, "Traveller, give way to the King!" as Laius is driving through the narrow place in his chariot, Oedipus boils up with rage and strides forward on his way without a word. One of the King's horses treads on his foot, and the old King also strikes him on the head from the chariot with the forked goad which he uses to drive his team. In a violent fury, and not knowing whom he is striking, Oedipus kills his father dead with his staff, and the herald as well.

In his lonely wanderings, he finally comes to Thebes. There the Sphinx is carrying off the young men and strangling them. She will cease doing so only if someone can find the right answer to a riddle she asks, "What creature is it which first goes on four, then on two and eventually on three?" Creon, the brother of Jocasta, has made the proclamation that Jocasta and the kingdom shall be his who overcomes the Sphinx. Oedipus finds the answer to the riddle—which is man, who as a child walks on all fours, as an adult on two legs, and in his old age on three (with a cane). The Sphinx throws herself into the sea, the city of Thebes is saved, and Oedipus becomes king and marries his mother, Jocasta.

After Oedipus has ruled for sixteen years, the city is visited by a terrible plague. Not only are men dying throughout the country, but the flocks and birds and the fruits of the field are blasted as well. The old blind prophet, Theiresias, reveals that the plague is the punishment for the twofold crime which Oedipus has committed, that of parricide and incest. When Oedipus realizes what he has unknowingly done, he blinds himself, and Jocasta commits suicide. The tragedy ends as Oedipus prepares for his banishment.

REJECTION OF OEDIPUS BY PARENTS

The Oedipus myth begins with a disruption, namely, the splitting off of the child from his parents. The orphaned child motif[1] is an important theme in many hero myths and fairy tales. "The child-god," says Kerènyi, "is usually an abandoned foundling."[2] However, the abandoned child is usually found alone in nature, as if born out of Mother Nature, or it is abandoned out of necessity to save its life. The child who is abandoned through rejection by the parents, and especially rejection by the mother, is not a common hero motif. This rejection

---

1. C. G. Jung and C. Kerènyi, *Essays on a Science of Mythology*, New York: Pantheon Books, 1949.

2. *Ibid.*, 38.

by the personal parents places the heroic destiny of Oedipus in a rather special category, which brings him very close to modern man. Since a negative relationship to one, and usually, both parents seems to be a rather consistent finding in neurosis, especially in the experience of rejection, we must find the connection.

Oedipus was rejected out of fear of incest and parricide on the part of his parents. Every primitive man fears incest more than any other crime, yet he does not reject his children. The "primitive" does not suffer from shame and guilt about his incestuous desires. Instead he arranges his culture around forms and rituals which minimize the danger of incest. The King and Queen of Thebes, Laius and Jocasta, might have understood the warning from Delphi as an indication of something wrong with the incest regulations in the Kingdom. When they chose to eliminate Oedipus, the incest fear proved to be a stronger power than the love for their child. Or, seen in another way, the natural and spontaneous parental love feelings are obstructed out of fear of incest. The "primitive" arranges culture so that there is a maximum of love and a minimum of incest. This is difficult since the more loving is the relationship between kin, the stronger is the desire for physical and sexual closeness. The strong measures which primitives must take to prevent incest is shown by their complex kinship arrangements and rites.

The fact that Oedipus believed his substitute parents to be his real parents points to a lack of conscious differentiation between the personal and archetypal parents. While the incest taboo functions to prevent concrete incest, it serves to promote symbolic or spiritual incest with the mother substitute.[3] Oedipus' unconsciousness, therefore, causes him to cut himself off from his substitute parents (the archetypal pair of opposites united in the image of the Royal Marriage or *hierosgamos),* out of fear of violating the incest prohibition. As a consequence there is no possibility of Oedipus finding fulfillment of his incestuous longings, except concretely.

---

3. C. G. Jung, *Symbols of Transformation, CW 12,* New York: Pantheon, 1956, § 332.

The psychoanalytic view that the resolution of the Oedipus complex lies in abandoning one's incestuous wishes is, in effect, what Oedipus did by removing himself forever from the King and Queen of Corinth. This eventually results in a concrete violation of the incest taboo, rather than preventing it. In contrast to the Freudian view, Jung has the following to say regarding the image of the Royal Marriage:

> I can do no more than demonstrate the existence of this image and its phenomenology. What the union of opposites really "means" transcends human imagination. Therefore the worldly-wise can dismiss such a "fantasy" without further ado, for it is perfectly clear *tertium non detur.* But that doesn't help us much, for we are dealing with an eternal image, an archetype, from which man can turn away his mind for a time, but never permanently. Whenever this image is obscured, his life loses its proper meaning and consequently its balance. So long as he knows that he is the carrier of life and that it is therefore important for him to live, then the mystery of his soul lives also—no matter whether it be conscious or unconscious. But if he no longer sees the meaning of his life in its fulfillment, and no longer believes in *man's eternal right to such fulfillment,* then he has betrayed and lost his soul, substituting for it a madness which leads to destruction, as our time demonstrates all too clearly.[4] (Italics mine)

THE FATHER COMPLEX

Isolated and alienated, Oedipus begins to wander. Having lost his connection to a fundamental unifying and organizing principle of the psyche, he becomes an easy victim of his unconscious emotions and passions. His only defense against the irrational dark forces in his own nature, is the cold pure light of his reason, the ego. In his very first encounter he is overcome with a rage which results in the slaying of his real father. One could interpret this as a deep, unconscious resentment toward the father for having betrayed

---

4. C. G. Jung, *Mysterium Coniunctionis, CW 14*, New York: Pantheon, § 201.

him, and for being largely responsible for his present state of wretchedness, rather than as an unconscious wish to eliminate father and marry mother.

My own experience working analytically with men has been that the conscious or unconscious resentment toward the father which usually exists, is primarily owing to the fact that their fathers failed them by not guiding them into a proper rite of transition into their own manhood. M. -L. von Franz has put it very well when she says, "If the images of the father and of the son are hostile opponents this means that something has gone wrong. The process of transformation has become blocked."[5]

It is true that the Old King must die, but this is part of a Rite of Renewal, not a hostile act. Whenever there is an unconscious slaying of the father—this also applies to modern dreams—this has a negative effect on the spiritual development of the son. Nevertheless, behind the slaying of the father is the motif of renewal, even if it does take a negative form.

THE SPHINX

Oedipus next encounters the Sphinx as his wanderings lead him to Thebes. As Great Mother she is also the protector of the feminine mysteries. We must inquire into the nature of the sin against the Great Mother, which has caused Her to punish the city of Thebes by devouring the young men. Jocasta's rejection of her child and her submission to the rational arguments of the masculine, was a violation of the Great Mother, of the feminine principles of love and relatedness. We have suggested that something was seriously wrong with the forms

---

5. M. -L. von Franz, "Uber Religiose Hintergrunde des Puer-Aeternus-Problems," *The Archetype*, Proceedings of the 2nd International Congress for Analytical Psychology, (trans. von Franz) Basel: S. Karger, 1964, 146.

and rituals regulating incest[6] in Thebes, and that this was the origin of the oracle's prediction of the disaster of incest and parricide. I feel that the incest taboo serves to promote human love and psychological development by gradually channelizing impersonal and phallic sexuality into the service of Eros. The cultural breakdown in Thebes, therefore, could be related to a neglect and devaluation of the feminine principle and the feminine mysteries. The second and third parts of the Sophocles trilogy would seem to substantiate this view. Thus the young men must be sacrificed to the Earth Mother until the feminine mysteries are reactivated and reintegrated.

It is hard to believe that Oedipus really gave the right answer to the riddle of the Sphinx, and the tragic developments which follow should confirm our suspicions. Almost any clever child, with a bit of thought, can come up with the answer given by Oedipus. I believe Oedipus missed an opportunity to redeem himself and the city of Thebes, by the sensible and accurate logic of his answer. Since the Great Mother cannot be destroyed, her death indicates either a process of transformation or repression. Subsequent events point to the latter possibility, since she continued to perform her tragic task even though she had disappeared from the face of the earth. Of the destruction of the Sphinx, Nietsche said, "He who by his wisdom hurls nature into the abyss of annihilation, has also experienced in himself the dissolution of Nature."

What, then, was the meaning of the riddle of Sphinx? Kerènyi suggests that Oedipus "recognized himself in the strange creature

---

6. In support of this thesis are Plato's views on incest. He indicates, in the following quotation, that no special rites or forms were necessary for the regulation of the incest desire. Our modern knowledge of the unconscious would surely cause us to question Plato's psychological insight into this matter. "When anyone has a brother or sister who is fair: and about a son or daughter the same unwritten law holds, and is a perfect safeguard so that no open or secret connection ever takes place between them. Nor does the thought of such a thing ever enter at all into the minds of most of them . . . (Relations of this type) are unholy, hated by the God and most infamous: and is not the reason of this that no one has ever said the opposite . . . (Italics mine) Plato, *Laws*, 838 D.

which the Sphinx meant by her riddle, but not what man is."[7] There are two lines of the riddle which support this view.

> On two feet, yet on four, there treads the earth,
> Yea, and on three, a creature of one name.
> *Alone it changes shape of all that walk;*
> *On ground or fly in air or swim the sea.*
> But when it goes supported on four feet,
> Then is the speed the feeblest in its limbs.[8]

Lines three and four would emphasize the process of transition, of rebirth and transformation, which belongs to the realm of the Great Mother and the Feminine Mysteries. I suggest that the rites and regulations surrounding incest also belong to the most ancient and fundamental of the woman's mysteries.

THE RENEWAL OF THE OLD KING

As a reward, or rather consequence, of having unconsciously slain his father and the Sphinx, Oedipus falls into an unconscious concrete incestuous relationship with his mother. He has simply replaced the old King, but there has been no renewal. In his *Mysterium Coniunctionis* Jung has dealt extensively with the image of the old King. "This figure represents the *prima materia* which ought to be transformed; the alchemists often describe him as being deficient, unredeemed, petrified or ill, or even sometimes evil, in the beginning of their opus. His deficiency consists mainly in an exaggerated egocentricity and of a 'hardening' of the heart, which later has to be dissolved in the alchemical bath. The old king is also frequently characterized by a great desire for power and a general concupiscentia."[9] Regarding the relationship between the old King and his Son (*puer aeternis*), von Franz, following Jung, says that they are not really opposites or opponents but actually one. "The alchemists

---

7. C. Kerènyi, *The Heroes of the Greeks*, New York: Grove Press, 1960, 99.
8. *Ibid.*, 98 (my italics).
9. von Franz, *The Archetype*, 145.

even called their substance *senex et puer,* (old man and boy). [Christ too was called old man *and* boy because he is the 'Ancient of Days' himself who was reborn as a child from the womb of the Virgin]. By dissolving him in their own opus, be it by fire or by water, the alchemists dissolved the senex into chaotic matter and dismembered him, after which he was transformed into the son."[10]

The Sphinx waits for Oedipus to come because he alone carries the hope of renewal, but he had lost touch with the mystery when he unconsciously slew his father. Before the Old King, the Father, is ready to die, it is necessary that he pass on the knowledge of the renewal rites to the Son. The father, as old wise man, represents a masculine principle which is the carrier of ancient wisdom and meaning. Though he may be lacking virility and phallic potency, it is through him that the son receives instruction in the rites of transition and rebirth.

Oedipus became a hero through the phallic power of his rational mind, but he was one of the most foolish of kings, because he lacked the wisdom that the phallic power must submit to the transforming power of Eros. Regarding the essentially phallic nature of Oedipus, Kerènyi links his name, which means "swollen foot," to the phallic Dactyls, one of the earth-born sons of the Great Mother. Oidyphallos, he says, would have been his name in the oldest times.[11]

The crime which is committed by the violation of the incest taboo is that undifferentiated phallic sexuality is gratified too soon and too easily, before the transforming principle of Eros has had a chance to develop. There is no mention of love in the marriage between Oedipus and his mother. Thus the city of Thebes falls under the domination of a masculine power principle, and reason is cut off from the source of life and renewal. The phallic power soon begins to wither on its cut vine, and the kingdom is threatened with becoming a desolate wasteland. The priest of Zeus tells Oedipus,

---

10. von Franz, *The Archetype*, 146.
11. Kerènyi, *The Heroes of the Greeks*, 93.

THE OEDIPUS MYTH AND THE INCEST ARCHETYPE

For the city, as thou thyself seest, is now too sorely vexed, and can no more lift her head from beneath the angry waves of death; a blight is on her in the fruitful blossoms of the land, in the herds among the pastures, in the barren pangs of women; and withal the flaming god, the malign plague, hath swooped on us, and ravages the town; by whom the house of Cadmus is made waste, but dark Hades rich in groans and tears.[12]

Oedipus finally receives a message from the oracle of Phoebus Apollo, telling him that the cleansing and healing of Thebes depends on finding the murderer of Laius and banishing him from the land; he does not know that he himself is this murderer. The fact that Apollo does not appear to demand punishment of Jocasta for her incestuous crime may be of some significance. Or, perhaps, the healing god is only concerned with breaking up the mother-son incest. However, since both parties must generally share the guilt and punishment for having violated the incest prohibition, this explanation does not seem satisfactory.

THE GREAT MOTHER AND INCEST

It is puzzling that Apollo fails to mention the crime of incest and reveals the crime of parricide as the cause of the plague. One would have expected the violation of the incest prohibition to be the more serious offense. Why does not the god demand punishment of Jocasta? I am unable to come to any conclusive answer to this question, but it is possible that it is the unredeemed phallic power which Oedipus represents that needs to be eliminated or transformed. This becomes especially meaningful if we consider that the deity responsible for the barrenness which has descended upon Thebes is probably the Great Mother. Her main concern is with fertility and fruitfulness, with death, rebirth, and transformation. The mother of all the gods has great compassion for all those who violate the incest taboo, for she more than any other knows the power which the incestuous attraction exerts over

---

12. Sophocles, "Oedipus The King," *The Tragedies of Sophocles*, London: Cambridge UP, 1928, 4.

85

both gods and men. Not only is she the worst offender herself, but it is she who evokes the eternal longing in man for incestuous union. We must not forget that to no other creature or god is incest forbidden— only to humanity. This is humanity's burden, but through it we have discovered the mystery of creativity and have become a partner with the Great Mother in her eternally creative process. We alone of all the creatures "that walk on ground or fly in air or swim the sea" can be transformed and reborn through the secret we have learned. The Great Mother is not offended by incest. In fact she demands the total submission of all her phallic sons to her insatiable need to be fertilized. What offends her most is the refusal of the masculine principle to enter into her eternal creative and repetitive cycle. Oedipus is the one who has lost all conscious connection to the Mothers, and he there- fore represents a negative phallic principle which is destructive to life.

We are forced to reevaluate the nature of Oedipus' incestuous crime. From the point of view of the Great Mother, his crime was his conscious resistance to incest, his denial of his incestuous longings. The fact that he committed incest unconsciously means that his conscious ego was not involved; or, to put it another way, the logos principle and the rational mind remained detached and uninvolved. Incest implies a total union of the opposites of the masculine and feminine principles. Where there is not total involvement, fertilization cannot occur, and the creative process stops. The eternal feminine is unable to resist the powerful need to be fertilized through the incestuous union. There is an indication that Jocasta did not abhor incest, for she tries to persuade Oedipus to leave off his investigation even though it is apparent that she already realizes that he is her son. Incest is not destructive to life but to the spiritual development of man. The violation of the incest taboo does not stop the eternal cycle of creativity, but it does interfere with humanity's own transformation. On the other hand, when the masculine principle of rational conscious- ness refuses to submit to the feminine principle of life, this results in sterility and destruction.

INCEST AND CONSCIOUSNESS

If it were up to the feminine life principle, it is doubtful that the incest taboo would have become such a powerful force in the human psyche. It would seem that the incest prohibition must have arisen out of some phallic or masculine principle reaching toward consciousness and individuality. The problem is that if the mystery of life and creativity lies in incest, how can these vital life forces continue if incest is forbidden? Jung gave us part of the answer when he emphasized that incest must take place on a symbolic or spiritual level. But this is no simple matter, for it usually involves a highly complex and evolved system of knowledge, ritual and instruction. The carriers of all this secret lore are the old wise men of the tribe, the medicine men, the Fathers. It is interesting, and I think important, that the guardians of the secret knowledge having to do with the feminine mysteries of death, rebirth, and transformation should be masculine. But is this not in itself indicative of the way in which the masculine spirit submits to the feminine life principle in a transforming way? The feminine is life, but it is the masculine logos principle which must point the way to new forms. "In the beginning was the Word . . . ."

I recall the dream of a woman patient in which a father was preparing his daughter for intercourse. His daughter was lying on a bed and he was examining her vagina and talking to her. The dreamer felt this dream made good sense, and she expressed the wish that her own father had given her such instruction. At that time, I felt that this was the mother's task, even though in the dream the mother of the girl was approving of the father's action. It is clear to me now that my patient's dream was pointing to the deep need she had to be instructed into the mystery of spiritual intercourse with a man, and with the masculine. Although she had been married for twenty years, she had no real personal relationship with her husband. This was primarily because she lived in darkness and ignorance regarding the nature, meaning, and mystery behind her repressed incestuous longings. It is the Father, as the carrier of traditional knowledge and meaning, who must initiate both males and females into the fundamental human mystery of spiritual transformation, which is behind the incest prohibition. Feminine wisdom is a continual affirmation of life, through its eternal readiness to respond to the quick of the moment; it is not communicated by the word and rite, but through presence and being.

Let us now return to Oedipus and the complex he represents. So far we have arrived at the following conclusions: 1) The abandonment of Oedipus by his parents is indicative of a cultural breakdown in the regulation of incest and rites of transition. 2) One of the consequences of this is the lack of differentiation between the personal and archetypal parents. Because of this, the fear of concrete incest and parricide forces Oedipus to cut himself off from the archetypal parents as represented by the King and Queen of Corinth. 3) The image of the Royal Marriage, the Brother-Sister incest, is a fundamental symbol which contains the mystery of the union of the opposites and spiritual transformation. Without a connection to this image, consciousness becomes a destructive phallic weapon, continually cutting the ego off from life. 4) The ego then becomes inflated and identifies with the Apollonian principle of rationality, clarity and moderation, but the unconscious becomes charged with a Dionysian rage and frenzy which continually threatens to obliterate ego consciousness. 5) The unconscious resentment toward the personal father for his alienation and for not having initiated him into the mysteries of spiritual transformation, causes Oedipus to murder his father in a fit of rage. On another level, the renewal of the father (the Old King) demands his death and rebirth through the son, but if this is not realized consciously, "it happens all the same in the unconscious, but in a negative form."[14] With this final rejection of the father, Oedipus' identification with an oppressive phallic power principle is complete. Unconsciously, however, the Great Mother rules supreme. 6) His victory over the Sphinx is spurious and represents a further breach between ego consciousness and the unconscious. 7) With the repression and rejection of the feminine, the fundamental human need for incestuous union becomes unconscious, causing an internal split between mind and body, love and sex.

---

14. von Franz, *The Archetype*, 147.

THE OEDIPUS MYTH AND THE INCEST ARCHETYPE

RESTRICTION VS REPRESSION OF SEXUALITY

Unbridled and untamed sexuality is the greatest obstacle to the development of consciousness. But the repression and denial of instinctual sexuality results in a fatal alienation between the conscious and the unconscious, between logos and life, which ultimately leads to a total obliteration of consciousness. The Great Mother will tolerate ego consciousness only as long as it is dedicated to the service of the feminine principle of renewal through union. Thus Her victory over King Oedipus is final and conclusive when she provokes him to such a state of anguish and frenzy that he destroys his vision (consciousness).[15] A culture is not repressive when the regulations and rites surrounding the incest taboo are working effectively. It does not-interfere with the child's full experience of his infantile and childish sexuality. By marking off the parents and siblings as forbidden objects for sexual expression, it endows them with an aura of mystery and numinosity. While the child can let his instinctual animal nature guide him in his other relationships, the incest taboo forces him to maintain some distance from family and kin, and to learn certain cultural forms. Since it is the archetypal father and mother and brother and sister which he first experiences in relationship to his family, the taboo enables him to begin to establish ego boundaries and to experience the archetypal wonder of the non-ego world in all its "holy" otherness. It is in this experience of otherness that ego consciousness begins to differentiate itself from Nature. The child becomes aware of a spiritual connection between mother and father which unites the family unit, as opposed to the more natural and instinctual connection which he has with his playmates. Because of the taboo, a higher value becomes attached to the archetypal image of the harmonious union between the masculine and feminine principles, than to the spontaneous and unconscious activity of the instincts. For the child, the mystery of this higher union becomes associated with a restriction of his sexuality and other instinctual urges which constantly demand immediate gratification.

---

15. Of course this only cuts off his vision of the outer world; symbolically, this can be interpreted as a submission to inner reality—the soul.

Restriction is not repression. Sexuality is not prohibited except in relation to the parent or sibling of the opposite sex. This does not mean that the sexual desire toward the tabooed kin becomes insignificant. On the contrary, the love connection increases the desire for total union of the spirit and the flesh. The fact that there is no sexual restriction between mother and father is another mystery for the child, and the image of marriage begins to form in his psyche as the way to eventually fulfill his incestuous longings.

Thus the incest taboo accomplishes two things: By restricting instinctual sexuality it helps bring about a differentiation between the ego and the non-ego "other," which is fundamental for the development of consciousness, and at the same time it reveals the possibility for gratification of the incest need on a higher level. In this way, the archetypal image of the union between the masculine and feminine opposites is activated and experienced as a living reality by the child. And as Jung has shown, whenever this image of the Royal or Divine Marriage is obscured, "life loses its proper meaning and therefore its balance." Where there are inadequate incest regulations or violation, this central archetypal image of the *hierosgarnos* becomes distorted or lost to consciousness. Oedipus, like modern man, is doomed unless he can reconnect with this eternal image.

OEDIPUS AT COLONUS

It is remarkable how closely the path of redemption which Oedipus must travel in *Oedipus at Colonus,* parallels the individuation process that is associated with the second half of life, as described by C. G. Jung. With his brutal self-castrating act, King Oedipus finally submits to the darkness of the mother world. But unlike the priests of the Mother Cults, his is a sacrifice of the phallic-logos principle, rather than phallic sexuality. Still with blood stained face, he continues to rant,

> Apollo, friends, Apollo was he that brought these my woes to pass,
> these my sore, sore woes but the hand that struck the eyes was

none save mine, wretched that I am! Why was I to see when sight
could show me nothing sweet?[16]

Through this act which corresponds to a total *sacrificium
intellectus,* Oedipus submits to the guidance of his anima as represented by his daughter, Antigone. The scene opens as the blind
Oedipus, old and worn, enters Colonus in Attica from the west. Antigone is his guide. He has at last come to the goal of his long and
difficult journey, where Apollo had proclaimed he would find peace
and redemption. It is significant that Sophocles calls our attention to
the fact that Oedipus is coming from the west. This would be consistent with the movement of the sun-god hero, from west to east, in his
night sea journey or journey into the underworld. Here in this grove
sacred to the goddesses who avenged a mother, the Erinyes, Oedipus
will find his rest. When it was at last his time to go, Oedipus in full
confidence follows Hermes, the Guide of Souls, into the underworld
and disappears from the face of the earth. His grave, which would be
no ordinary grave, would hereafter protect the Athenians.[17] The ritual
of the descent into the underworld belongs to the Feminine Mysteries. There are other indications which link the final redemption of
Oedipus to the Mysteries of Demeter. The disciples of Orpheus, for
example, believe that Hades and Persephone are the parents of the
Erinyes or Eumenides, the Benevolents.[18] And Aeschylus, in his story
of Oedipus, locates his grave in a sacred precinct of Demeter in
Eteonos.[19]

ANTIGONE

In *Antigone,* the conflict between the calcified Logos principle and
the Eros principle is most clearly demonstrated. Although *Antigone*
is generally placed last in this trilogy concerning the royal house of
Thebes, it was actually written and performed much earlier (442 B.C.)

---

16. Sophocles, "Oedipus The King," *The Theban Plays,* 51.
17. Kerenyi, *The Heroes of the Greeks,* 103.
18. C. Kerenyi, *The Gods of the Greeks,* London: thames and Hudson, 1951, 47.
19. Kerenyi, *Heroes,* 104.

than *Oedipus Rex* (429) or *Oedipus at Colonus* (401). This chronological order has greater psychological validity than the usual narrative order.

The play begins after the sons of Oedipus kill each other in bitter combat. Polynices had stormed the seven gates of Thebes with his Argive allies. His brother, Eteocles, was defender of the city. Thebes withstood the attack and Creon, now master of the city, resolves to make an example of the iniquity of the invader: Polynices' body is ordered to be left unburied and unmourned. The penalty for disobedience is death by stoning. Sophocles does not make Creon into a villan, but rather a sincere and honorable man concerned about his responsibility for the integrity of the state. The slain traitor is Antigone's brother. When no man will defy the order, and the king holds rigidly to his position, Antigone takes it upon herself to give her brother a proper burial even though it means her death. The tragedy does not end here, because the king's son is betrothed to Antigone. The son (Haemon) wants desperately to hold onto his loyalty and respect for his father, but in the end he cannot accept the hard-hearted erosless principles which Creon rigidly maintains. Haemon then takes his own life.

The problem of the renewal of the rigid old king through the son appears once again in this earlier drama. The death of the son, rather than the father as in *Oedipus Rex,* extinguishes all hope for renewal and redemption. Eros cannot survive when all opposition to the calcified logos principle is destroyed. In the end Creon even loses his wife to her own hand. And the play closes with this choral ode:

Of happiness the crown
And chiefest part
Is wisdom, and to hold
The gods in awe.
This is the law
That, seeing the stricken heart
Of pride brought down,
We learn when we are old.[20]

20. Sophocles, "Antigone," *The Theban Plays*, Baltimore: Penguin Books, 1947, 162.

THE OEDIPUS MYTH AND THE INCEST ARCHETYPE

The drama which unfolds in *Antigone*, brings us into immediate contact with the tragic life destroying consequences of a state or condition in which Logos is not functioning in the service of Eros. Then in *Oedipus Rex*, a deep elaboration of the problem can be seen, in which the incestuous origins of this disharmony between Logos and Eros is revealed. *Oedipus at Colonus*, which was probably written in the last years of the poet's life, points to the path of redemption and renewal through a descent into the underworld, and initiation into the feminine mysteries. Here, at last, there is hope that the incest archetype, the *hierosgamos,* will be re-activated, and that this central symbol of union and wholeness will be brought back into consciousness.

CONCLUSION

The Oedipus myth indicates that the vital meaning of the incest taboo had fallen into the unconscious and was functioning autonomously, instead of being dealt with consciously and creatively. This is even true in our times. Consequently, the moral confiict which rightfully belongs to the mystery of incest has become focused on the need to gain control over the spontaneous instinctual reaction, especially sexuality. When the repression of instincts becomes necessary in a culture, it is a sign that something has gone wrong with the collective institutions for the regulation of incest. This produces a mind/body split, and power, avarice, infantilism, and lust become the dominant features of such a culture, rather than a love and kinship connection. The development of Eros seems to be dependent on both the incest taboo and the longing for incest. The taboo enables the child gradually to bring his untamed instinctual urges and energies into the service of Eros, but only if he believes that through this process he will eventually find fulfillment of his deep need for incestuous union.

PART THREE

Phallos

CHAPTER EIGHT

Phallos and Masculine Psychology

Masculine and Feminine are qualities of the human personality common to both sexes. But a man's nature tends to be more rooted in a Phallic spirit, while a woman's tends to emerge out of a Womb spirit.

The Phallic spirit, like the penis, functions autonomously, independent of control by the rational mind. One might argue that the reactions of the penis are subject to rational control, but this is dubious. Although the penis can apparently be manipulated to perform, without doubt it has a will of its own which resists all the trickery of the rational mind (ego) if it so desires. Furthermore, men who habitually employ the ego to control the reactions of the penis accomplish this by varying degrees of numbing detachment. Ultimately the phallic spirit in the penis responds to such treatment by causing some form of psychological or physiological impotency. Obviously, the control of the ego over the penis is minimal and of limited duration. However, the attitude and relationship of ego to penis can effect profound changes in the reactions of this primary organ of masculine sexuality.

The sudden uncontrollable surge of blood into the penis, causing it to stand erect, is a great mystery. The desire behind it may be love for another, or it may also be pure lust or desire for power over another, or it may be a mixture of all these elements. Often the penis becomes aroused by sexual fantasies having no relationship to an actual person. And at times, a sudden erection totally unrelated to sexual desire will occur, which suggests that the phallic rush of energy into the penis is a spirit which transcends the sexual drive. A few examples may help clarify this point: men often awaken from sleep with an erection and without sexual desire, but with thoughts related to work, ideas, sports, and other activities. (One traditional but disproven explanation of this phenomenon is that it is caused by bladder pressure.) It is not uncommon for a man at the height of an exciting nonsexual challenging experience to suddenly find himself with an erection.

If we accept the idea of the penis as an organ under the influence of the phallic spirit, we can deduce something about the nature of this God, Phallos. We recognize, above all, its essentially unpredictable quality. Experientially, it seems to manifest itself as a sudden powerful surge or thrust from within, flowing rapidly with the desire to make contact with another object—be it idea, image, another person or an inanimate object. While it is the desire of the feminine Womb spirit to be entered, to receive and embrace, the desire of Phallos is to move toward penetration of an unknown realm. Phallos therefore is fundamental to human initiative. Without it we can be moved, but we cannot move. Anyone who fears being moved out of old stabile structures into areas that are new, unknown, and unformed, will fear the sudden, irrational influx of Phallos. Consequently, the right relationship to this spirit is essential for change and psychological development. At the same time, it is a spirit constantly on the move: curious, impulsive, explosive, daring but incapable of commitment; filled with the joy of its own power and ready to use it against anything that gets in its way, unconcerned with tending and nourishing human relationships unless tempered and contained in Eros. When women complain about men only wanting to get into their pants and not caring about the relationship, they are really speaking of Phallos. When a mother is unable to cope with the constant activity, playful curiosity and demands of her child, she is often suffering from a bad relationship to Phallos.

I recall a young mother who was having great difficulty with her unmanageable male child; she dreamt that her son was zigzagging and bouncing off the walls of his room with such velocity that she constantly had to duck in order to keep from getting hit. Suddenly he became a huge Phallos, and she awakened terrified. Obviously this woman was in a bad relationship to Phallos. A boy's relationship to the phallic root of his masculine nature will be profoundly influenced by a mother so threatened and judgmental in her attitude toward his essential maleness.

Love and Phallos are often difficult to differentiate because both are active, initiating life forces. Both are experienced as a force moving one away from where one is, toward another object or person. Furthermore, the Goddess of Love is believed to have been born out of the severed genitals of the Sky God, Ouranos. No doubt there is a close relationship between Phallos and Love. Perhaps Phallos is the primal source of the energy contained in every emotion that motivates a person to move, to act, to initiate. Since Love is primarily a great movement toward union with another, it too must be rooted in Phallos.

Still, Love and Phallos are not identical. How do they differ? Perhaps the main difference is that Love is always a desire to merge, to unite, while Phallos is primarily a desire to penetrate and explore. In addition, Love always evokes great concern for preserving the beauty and integrity of the other, while Phallos lacks such concern; in its pure form it tends to rape and ultimately destroy the object of its fascination. Love, though a powerfully active and penetrating force, is enormously sensitive and receptive. In other words it combines both a masculine and feminine principle. Nevertheless, Love in its primitive Aphroditic state, is predominantly phallic. This makes untransformed Love fickle, incapable of commitment, unconcerned with tending and nourishing a permanent human relationship, ready to move so soon as it has achieved its goal of union. Love needs Eros before it becomes capable of taking care of human relationships, but we must leave discussion of this important issue until Part IV.

Clearly Phallos is the source of all of humanity's creative energies. It is a force which always moves away from the old, from what is, toward the new and unknown. Phallic curiosity is the activating principle behind humanity's creative imagination, but the penetrating, dissecting quality of curiosity becomes destructive and antihuman without Eros to preserve the integrity and mystery of the unknown object.

Phallos, the generative source of life, is pure emotion, pure desire. Any thought, impulse, image or idea is brought to life by Phallos. It is pure spirit, pure energy using anything and everything as its material for giving shape to the creative urge. In its insatiable hunger to fertilize and create new forms, it has neither awareness nor concern for human limitations. Without Phallos nothing moves, nothing changes. Fear of Phallos results in fragmentation and stasis. I must be open and desirous to receive Phallos or it cannot enter me. Consequently, if I do not have the right relationship to the receptive feminine qualities of my soul, my womb is closed, and I begin to dry up because I cannot be fertilized and renewed by Phallos. The womb, receptive earth, is, therefore, primary. Without it the Life Force has no vessel to receive it, and the blood of my own life will soon cease to flow. Death.

Let us return now to the woman who was so threatened by her son's phallic qualities. The inner image of the archetypal feminine is largely shaped by a man's experience of his mother. Typically, most Western men experience the receptive maternal aspects of their own psyche as rejecting of Phallos. How could it be otherwise? Everything we know about the ancient feminine mysteries indicates that they were centered around the worship of Phallos. Modern woman is as cut off from these mysteries as was Oedipus. Instead of her Eros, embracing and humanizing her son's potent phallic energies, she attempts to subdue and control this irrational spirit with her ego. So long as a man's internal image of the feminine is rejecting of Phallos, he can never come to a right relationship with his own creative spirit, and the same situation applies to women, as we shall see presently. Consequently, the inner feminine (the anima) must change before a man can truly open up to Phallos.

How does this negative experience of the feminine manifest itself internally and in life? In men's dreams, a frequent motif is the sudden appearance of mother or a mother figure just as the dreamer is about to surrender to his sexual desires. *Mother inhibits Phallos.* Since mother is also associated with soft, tender, loving feelings, and Phallos is the source of all passion, a man has great difficulty getting his passion together with his love when his experience of the mother archetype is so castrating. More often than not, this same archetypal pattern will be constellated in relationship to his wife. I have often heard a woman express her pain about not being able to be physically close and tender with her husband because when she does he immediately wants to fuck. And I have often heard a man complain about how his wife says no to sex after having aroused him with physical intimacy. This common dilemma is a clear indication that both partners are suffering from the same negative relationship to Phallos. Should the woman yield to her husband's sexual passion, she knows the close tender feelings will be obliterated, for she, too, is plagued from within by this rejecting maternal archetype.

A young man complaining about just such an experience with his wife had the following dream: "Jane [his wife] and I were being very loving, but as soon as I wanted to fuck her, she froze up and said no. I was furious. Then I was with Sue. We weren't close, but I was turned on sexually. I was surprised when she put her hand on my penis and expressed her desire for sex." Let us briefly explore this dream. He described Sue as aggressive, masculine, hard, and domineering. He felt his wife was soft and feminine. How clearly this dream illustrates my thesis: Mother-Wife is soft, tender, loving but rejecting of Phallos; a hard, masculinized female cut off from Eros can embrace Phallos, but only because she herself has rejected the maternal roots of her femininity. The results are loveless sex and passionless love.

Paralyzed by his fear, rejection, and repression of Phallos, another man was plagued by threatening nightmares. Night after night he struggled to escape the angry, demonic phallic forces within his psyche: snakes, crocodiles, sharks, Nazis, Communists, black men, the Mafia, etc. Threatening dreams generally reflect the dreamer's conscious attitude toward vital aspects of his personality, which are expressed symbolically in the dream imagery. The phallic symbolism in this man's dreams is obvious, so we can assume that his conscious attitude is hostile and rejecting of Phallos. It should not surprise us to find that his relationship to his mother had been unusually close, but that she had denied and discouraged the expression of any of his phallic qualities. Instead she filled him with her own fantasies about the fame and fortune that would one day be *given* to him. He was the chosen one, sensitive, and loving. Everything would come to him because of his goodness. Did he not see how different he was from his crude, aggressive, uneducated, domineering father? And so on. So long as this now internalized mother remains unchanged, there is no possibility of Phallos being embraced and humanized by Eros.

Clearly the experience with the mother will largely determine a child's relationship to his/her own irrational nature. But what about the father? Does a child not also experience a father as loving and embracing? Of course a child does or should. Is it not possible, then, that a man could experience the Mother archetype negatively and still be able to be receptive to his own spirit through the Father archetype? Yes, fathers often assume the positive archetypal mother role. When this happens, however, the child is generally robbed of the essential experience of the positive father archetype. Although the development of a child is largely dependent on the experience of both parents as loving and accepting, there is a difference between paternal and maternal love.

Maternal love is primarily concerned with nourishing and supporting the mysterious internal life processes which slowly shape the child into a unique creation. As a specific function, the Maternal (not mother) is not particularly concerned with instructing the child about the ways of the world, except to make the child aware of outer realities which might endanger its development. In other words, the maternal quality functions largely to support the child's positive connection to its own soul or spirit. It is inner-directed. Psychologically, the positive Mother archetype is experienced as that wonderful human quality which is totally accepting of one's nature.

PHALLOS AND MASCULINE PSYCHOLOGY

The Father archetype (not father) expresses itself primarily in Logos. Logos is the active principle behind human thought and reason, often considered to be identical to the Word. It is the principle behind all human and cosmic order. Wisdom, justice, law, and human consciousness are all manifestations of Logos. Both Anaxagoras and Philo believed Logos to be an intermediary between the Deity and humanity.[1] In Christian theology, Christ is believed to be the incarnation of Logos. Since Eros also functions as an intermediary between the Divine and human, perhaps it is more closely related to Logos than we have realized. In fact, in the person of Christ, Eros and Logos would seem to be united.

As an expression of paternal love, Logos is concerned with guiding and supporting the child's spirit in relationship to the world. In this sense it is outer and other directed. A man lacking a good connection to this archetype will have difficulty in his relationship to the world, to outer reality. If, for example, he was fortunate enough to have a positive experience of the Mother archetype, he may have great acceptance of his own nature and spirit, but he will still have enormous difficulties establishing a positive connection to others and outer reality.

Logos is an uniquely human attribute but so is Eros. Perhaps Eros is the force behind the desire and experience of human love and creative union, while Logos is the capacity to formulate, to derive universal principles out of such experiences. In so far as Logos desires to penetrate and explain the mysteries of cosmic order, it is related to Phallos, but in its desire to produce forms for creative human intercourse, it is related to Eros.

The Father archetype (Logos) is responsible for those qualities which enable the individual to be stable, to withstand the disrupting storms and pressures of life, to be steadfast and committed to something beyond the immediate and personal. Without a positive connection to this archetype, an individual lacks the inner strength, perseverance, and stability to stand alone, to endure the tensions of living which are so essential for psychological development.

---

1. James Hatings (ed.), *Encyclopedia of Religion and Ethics*, Vol. 8, Edinburgh: T.&T. Clark, 1953, 134-35.

When Logos, the Father, becomes rigid, and no longer creatively serves human life and development, the situation is experienced as oppressive. Logos must always be in the service of the human connection, Eros. The existing dichotomy between Logos and Eros is simply another manifestation of the prevailing soul-splitting mind/ body dichotomy. Logos/Eros is really one archetype, one function.

The identification of Logos with the rational mind is either a cause or a consequence of the Logos/Eros split. The capacity of the rational mind (ego) to detach itself from bodily feelings and emotions, to anesthetize itself to bodily sensations, to cut itself off from life, to become an observing disembodied eye, is not how Logos works. Logos is deeply involved with and rooted in life. Although it uses the rational mind's capacity for detachment, it never loses connection to the generative life source from which it gets its power. Thus Logos is rooted in Phallos. When cut off from its Phallic root, the rational mind takes over as a poor and impotent substitute. Without Logos the rational mind lacks strength and vitality. It soon withers to become a rigid, atrophied, pompous pretense of Logos. Not for nothing have the youth been compelled to "blow their minds" with drugs.

Logos is not necessarily more rational than Phallos. It has the same dynamic potency to explore, to penetrate, to overcome obstacles, and to understand the unknown, as does Phallos. It can appear as suddenly and impulsively, and with the same numinosity, as does Phallos. It can overwhelm. Only in its capacity to restrain, in its cultivation and commitment, does it differ essentially from Phallos. The true Logos cannot enter the soul so long as one fears Phallos.

Impotency—mental, spiritual, and physical—is the consequence of a man's inability to embrace Phallos. Nothing will alter his basic feeling of inadequacy until he overcomes his fear of Phallos as it begins to stir, to rise up numinously at the root of his being. It is different for a woman. As long as she feels connected to the softness and receptivity of her womb, she will feel womanly—unless her soul is dissatisfied with living only the archetypal feminine. However any woman who has a need to think creatively, to become spiritually free of her dependency on a man, to individuate, will feel inadequate and unfulfilled until she, too, can allow the full potency of Phallos to enter consciousness. Still, a woman can lead a relatively full, if unconscious, life for many years before she is forced to come to grips with her fear of Phallos. A man cannot. It is essential for his initiation into manhood.

I remember a dream I had a number of years ago, which clearly reveals my relationship to Phallos at that time. I had been struggling with a difficult conflict for several weeks preceding the dream, and I was disgusted with my own impotency in the face of a situation which was demanding decisive action. The dream was in two parts:

> An aggressive, muscular man starts talking to my wife as she suns herself at the sea shore. He is wearing bikini trunks, and I can see his huge erection bulging through them. He moves toward my wife and pushes his cock close to her face. She says nothing, but I can see she is fascinated and aroused by this crude exhibitionistic bastard. I am furious, but even more so toward my wife for not sending him away. I leave in a rage. I am then in a dark room, and my head is filled with images of this man with my wife. Suddenly, in my imagination, she grabs his cock and lustfully begins fondling and sucking it. I am horrified to find myself becoming aroused by this fantasy, and I try to cut it off but to no avail. I feel I am about to have an orgasm and try even more desperately to stop the images. I can't. I awaken in a fury, deeply offended by the fact that my wife would respond so lustfully to a man who has no love for her.
>
> In the second dream I had to take my wife to some type of healing ritual, which was for women only. The healer started to massage her shoulders, but I noticed that his penis was hanging limply out of his pants. Once again I watched with interest wondering what my wife would do. I was pleased when I saw she was annoyed and disgusted. After telling the healer what I thought of him, I took my wife, and we left.

Viewing my wife as a receptive feminine aspect of myself, and the man as a symbol of my own primal aggressive phallic thrust, it seems obvious that I (ego) reject this part of myself. The fact that my wife (anima) embraces Phallos would certainly seem to be positive. But why is my ego attitude still so judgmental, fearful, and rejecting of Phallos?

When I left to enter into the dark room, it reminded me of the bedroom I had occupied during my early adolescence when I was having all those intensely lustful sexual fantasies about my sisters. This clearly reveals the incestuous origins of my fears about my own aggressive sexual nature. A subtle, but important point which the dream makes, is that I even feared surrendering to my sexual imagination as a consequence of my incest wound.

In the second dream, since my wife (anima) must undergo a healing ritual, it is possible that something is still wrong with her relationship to Phallos. We encounter an apparently impotent healer, but still he is the healer. There is no doubt that his limp penis hanging foolishly out of his pants is the main point. I have seen a number of women's dreams in which they are repulsed and indignant when confronted by a dream figure with an exposed, limp penis. These women have tended to demand that a man be always strong and potent, and to feel disdain, even fury toward a man who seemed weak and indecisive. Let us not divert our attention at this time to the problem of a woman's relationship to Phallos, but these women's dreams call attention to a not uncommon feminine response to masculine impotency.

When the generative life force (Phallos) is full and flowing, one might be fearful, but it is always awesome and fascinating. Phallos erect is to be respected. But Phallos is not always erect; the Life Force is not always flowing outward. Often it retreats or lies peacefully dormant. To love Phallos means not only to embrace one's potency but one's impotency. In my dream my wife rejects Phallos when it is foolish and impotent. Unless one can accept being weak, foolish, helpless, one will always fear the potent surge of Phallos. The other side of tumescence is detumescence. Phallos, like life, rushes in as a great flowing force, but life ebbs just as suddenly and rapidly as it flows. Thus my fear of embracing my phallic potency was probably owing to the fact that my anima was still rejecting of my impotency.

PHALLOS AND MASCULINE PSYCHOLOGY

Now that we have made the connection between the fear of phallic potency and the fear of impotency, we can discuss some important differences between masculine and feminine psychology. The inability to initiate effective action toward the realization of a desire tends to make a man feel impotent. He need not necessarily act so long as he feels the power to act. A woman tends to feel impotent mainly when she is *without* desire; at least this seems to be the case when she is connected to the ground of her womb-like nature. As long as a woman feels open to respond to the quick of life, she can, without feeling inadequate, accept her passivity as well as her incapacity to act effectively upon her desire. She may, of course, experience pain and frustration about her unfulfilled needs; however, her sense of potency is not as dependent on her power to act, but rather on the connection to her desire and the belief in her capacity to respond to its fulfillment. For example, a young, extremely passive woman lived for years in a state of isolation devoid of any relationship to a man. After months of analysis in which she refused to examine her relationship to men and sexuality, she finally revealed that she had felt nothing wrong with herself in these areas. Her sense of adequacy came from her fantasy that as soon as the right man came along she would be ready to receive him. This exposure of her identification with the princess of the Sleeping Beauty myth came as a consequence of her sudden realization that she would be incapable of responding to her Prince Charming even if he should appear. A man too, can live for years in a fantastic delusion about his potency. But his myth is that he has the power actively to effect the realization of his desire, and that he is only holding back until the time is right.

So, a man would seem to gather his sense of strength and potency from his capacity to act, while a woman's strength would seem to be more rooted in her desire to respond. The demand that Phallos be always erect and capable of asserting itself is naturally more prevalent among men than among women, although many women are plagued from within by a similar demand. A man will be continually undermined and spiritually crippled as long as he is caught in the equations: Erect Phallos = Potency; Limp Phallos = Impotency.

107

Furthermore, he is forced to escape into his fantastic delusions of phallic potency in order to maintain any sense of adequacy and self respect. Life for him becomes a series of evasions. He finds the realities of his existential condition and the non-phallic dimensions of his personality intolerably painful, so that the soul's authentic needs are forever slipping away from his grasp and left unfulfilled.

Our Western culture identifies progress and productivity with masculine vitality and strength. Productive = potent and creative; counterproductive = impotent and destructive. Clearly such attitudes reflect a misunderstanding and distortion of masculinity. A man can free himself of this phallic fixation only if he experiences and joyfully accepts those states of passive, unknowing, helplessness as expressions of his receptive feminine nature. Rather than shrivelling up with feelings of impotency, a man must be able to sink deeply into the *strength* of his own desire to be fertilized.

CHAPTER NINE

Phallos and Feminine Psychology

Nowadays, a man must be terribly foolish or terribly coura-geous to write about the psychology of women. Whichever it is, I have little choice since much of my understanding of the human psyche is an outcome of my concern about my own relationship to actual women, and equally to those vital, neglected feminine aspects of my own soul. When a man writes about feminine psychology, it is difficult to know how much of what he describes belongs to the experience of his own feminine soul (or anima), and how much to his accurate perceptions of archetypal dominants belonging to real flesh-and-blood women. One must always be alert to a man who projects his own fantasies on women when he speaks about their psychology. In order to help the reader sort out the wheat from the chaff in this chapter, let me expose some of my internal difficulties with the feminine which undoubtedly color my perceptions.

I have no memories of having had any close, warm physical contact with my mother during childhood, at least until about the age of twelve. Yet I have heard from my older siblings and relatives that my mother was quite physical with me. I was the youngest of seven children, born seventeen years after my mother's first son, who was followed by five girls. She had not wanted me and attempted to abort the pregnancy. Later, as I was told, she apparently attempted to atone for her guilt by being particularly loving and affectionate with me, so it seems probable that I have indeed repressed all memories of a physical connection to her. The relationship between my mother and father was very bad. In later years she complained about how terribly cold and detached he had always been, how he had never really respected her, and how he had just used her sexually. Also, in later years, my father expressed deep resentment toward my mother for having rejected him sexually, particularly after my birth. One can imagine that this new son may have given my mother a sense of renewal, and that she projected her soul-mate image onto him, and my father must have resented my intrusion like hell. So the incestuous triangle probably began early for me. I have no memories of my father being warm or loving toward me, at least not until I was in my teens. I do remember being generally fearful of him and of his beating me with his belt on several occasions.

This severe memory gap in relationship to my mother, plus only fearful memories of my father, suggest the classical Oedipus complex. When I was between the ages of seven to ten, one of my sisters involved me in periodic sex play, but I do not recall ever feeling aroused. Apparently I also experienced the typical latency period as described by Freud. However at about the age of twelve, I was invaded by intense sexual fantasies and desires, much of which was provoked by my sisters, as I mentioned in Chapter One. I would have had difficulty enough just handling the psychophysiological changes of puberty, but this business with my sisters was too much. No doubt my sisters were having their own incestuous problems in relationship to my parents.

Being unable to repress my sexuality, I repressed all loving feelings toward my sisters (which, as I have suggested, is one way a child can deal with the incest tension). On the other hand, I did have loving feelings, but no sexual feelings, toward my mother during adolescence. So there we are, the classic love/sex split of the incest wound. However, since the purely lustful, impersonal sexuality was directed toward my sisters, the pattern is not as clear as in the more typical case in which such virgin goddess archetypes as Mary or Artemis are projected onto mother and sister. Although I had little guilt about my sexual fantasies, I was overwhelmed with both the incest horror and the fear of castration from acting upon these desires in relation to my sisters.

110

PHALLOS AND FEMININE PSYCHOLOGY

All of this had a devastating effect on me, and it took me many years before I was able to bring my passionate impersonal sexuality into a loving connection with a woman. But the scar is still quite tender, and it still angers me when women are unconscious about their own unloving, uncaring, and impersonal sexuality, and then dump all that "dirty" sexual imagery onto men. In a more creative vein, my wound has led me to the insight that central to a woman's quest for individuation is her conscious relationship to Phallos and the development of her sexual imagination. This theme will form the main body of this chapter.

Every healthy woman has a deep need to submit to a benevolent phallic power, to receive and contain it. The instinctual feminine reaction (attraction, fascination, fear, and withdrawal) to the sword-like aggressive phallic power, has the effect of transforming the penis into an instrument which opens up a channel for the circulation of Eros. Without the help of her instincts, a woman is unable to mediate the union in love which she needs, and which the man also needs.

Fear and *withdrawal* seem to be inherent in the sexual instinct of the female (even among animals, it is a common pattern for the female to run away from the male—often in circles—after she has already selected him as her partner). While the cultural recognition and acceptance of woman's sexual needs has been important in overcoming Puritanism and nineteenth century morality, it has done little to bring her closer to her instincts. A woman who has no restraints upon her sexual desires is not necessarily any more in touch with her instinctual nature than the woman who rejects and represses her desire. If a woman submits to her attraction to a man before she feels contained in her love for him, she is generally not listening to and respecting her instinctual fear of Phallos. As a consequence, her natural fear and modesty move into the unconscious where they work destructively by making her feel distrustful and insecure. Her own sexuality then becomes phallic and unrelated, rather than open and receptive. Instead of loving the man and evoking love in him through the trembling contractions and expansions of her own desire to receive him, she becomes overwhelmed by her need for love and acceptance, which completely cuts the man off from his eros.

111

ROBERT STEIN

A woman must feel certain of her love before she feels safe to open her womb to receive the man. In the male, the instinctual sexual dominant moves toward penetration, not openness; a man does not, therefore, feel as psychologically exposed with his erect penis as does a woman with her sexual desire. In fact the symbolic phallic power and potency of the erect penis tends to make the man feel invulnerable. Surrender to his sexual desire is consequently not as dependent on his feeling contained and protected in an atmosphere of love. Of course this refers only to the basic instinctual dominants; on a more human level, men also need to be contained in love.

Henry Miller describes a blundering and pathetically comical sexual sequence in his book, *The World of Sex.*[1] He tells of a woman who would not permit him any form of sexual intimacy if it meant that she had to consciously acknowledge her own desires. He discovered that as long as he distracted her with inconsequential talk, she was wide open and responsive. But as soon as he inadvertently stopped his chatter and she was forced to become aware, she reacted with shock and indignation. By not allowing her own sexual fantasies to reach consciousness, such a woman also remains unconscious of her instinctual fear as well as of her desire; thus she is unable to communicate either her desires or her fears to the man, both of which are needed in order to evoke tender and loving feelings in him. Instead she resists him by numerous unconscious defense mechanisms which either provokes the man to forcefully break through the barriers or to completely reject her, if his desire is not sufficiently strong.

The sexual dilemma of the modern woman can be restated as follows: if she remains unconscious of her sexual desire for the male, she also remains unconscious of her fears of the phallic thrust and of the protective instincts most natural to her; she then defends herself by unconscious acts of aggression which, instead of evoking Eros in the male, have quite the opposite effect. On the other hand if she becomes conscious of her desire and willingly surrenders to her attraction before feelings of personal warmth and tenderness have had

---

1. Henry Miller, *The World of Sex*, Paris: Olympia Press, 1959.

time to develop, she, too, falls under the power of Phallos, losing her own connection to the uniting power of Eros. On a grand scale, women seem all too readily to have submitted to Phallos, in both its sexual and spiritual epiphanies. As a consequence we live in a hard and brutal phallic-dominated world, ruled by the big stick and the dividing sword. Phallos must be continually humanized by Eros or it is destructive.

As long as the masculine aspects of her psyche (the animus) force her to place a higher value on consciousness, objectivity, and reason than on Eros, a woman becomes cut off from her own nature. The animus must become a benevolent power which supports Eros as the humanizing principle before she can regain trust in the essential dignity and wholeness of her being. Without such trust she is unable to truly love a man because to open herself to him means to expose the fragile mysteries of her soul to phallic destructiveness.

Jung and many of his followers have shown that the animus is often experienced as negative because it is being neglected; because its needs for creative expression are being rejected. Women in analysis therefore are often encouraged to paint, to write, to read, to study, to give some concrete form and expression to the spiritual demands of the animus. The salutary effect of such activity, when it is a true reflection of the needs of the animus, is well established. By cooperating with the animus in this way, the woman begins to experience it as a positive creative aspect of her own being rather than as a negative, destructive force. She feels a widening of consciousness and a new sense of power and freedom when she is able to submit to her spiritual animus. This is especially true where a woman is under the domination of an animus which demands that she fulfill the masculine image of the all-nourishing, all-containing, impersonal Mother-Wife archetype.

In our culture, where the masculine logos principle is so cut off from the feminine archetype of life, there is a tremendous pressure from the unconscious for the ego to submit to the blissful oblivion of the incestuous union with the Great Mother. Because of this loss of connection with the Incest Symbol, modern woman is pressured from within and without to concretize this archaic image of the Great Mother who eternally cohabitates with her children; thus, a woman today begins to feel more of an individual when she rebels against this projection and becomes involved in creative work beyond the role of Mother. Betty Friedan, in her book, *The Feminine Mystique,*[2] and the Woman's Liberation Movement, clearly express this attitude. Unfortunately this solution does not bring a woman closer to her basic nature. The individuality and freedom she experiences is illusory or, at best, transitory and it does not enable her to open herself to Eros and experience a deep love connection with a man. In fact, a woman who is identified with the archetypal Mother-Wife is at least able to maintain her connection to love, even if it is love on the most primitive level and essentially impersonal.

What, then, is modern woman to do, caught between the Scylla of her spiritual animus and the Charybdis of an animus which demands that she reject consciousness and identify with the archetypal feminine? A woman unable to submit to either, usually a woman with a severe negative mother problem, finds herself paralyzed and cut off from both life and spirit. Where and how can she establish a connection with the positive and benevolent masculine principle which knows that the spiritual development of a woman rests upon the foundation of Eros? Let us once again return to the woman's relationship to her sexual instinct for our answer.

Psychic relatedness, Eros, is fundamental to a woman's sexuality. She cannot truly open herself psychically or sexually to the masculine if Eros is lacking; undifferentiated phallic sexuality does not need Eros to perform. We have discussed the importance of the basic feminine reaction of fear and withdrawal from the phallic aggressiveness of the male. This instinctual reaction on the part of the woman evokes the eros principle in the man, but only if the woman is able to communicate her basic attraction to his phallic potency; otherwise it either provokes him to even greater phallic activity or to total rejection of her. As long

2. Betty Friedan, *The Feminine Mystique*, New York: W. W. Norton & Company, 1963.

as a woman is unconscious of and rejecting of her own impersonal phallic sexuality, she will manifest these same attitudes in her actual relationships with men. Without doubt women have their share of undifferentiated and impersonal phallic sexuality. Why do they have such extreme difficulty in revealing and accepting this aspect of their nature? They certainly have no qualms about letting the impersonal opinions and judgements of the animus speak out.

Before the eros principle can regain its rightful place in the male-female relationship, a woman must come to a more positive, conscious connection to her own unrelated and aggressive sexuality. All those instinctual sexual urges and fantasies which are not personally or psychically related must be accepted and experienced *consciously*: the whole realm of infantile and childish sexuality; the desire to expose oneself which all children have in spite of an inherent feminine modesty; the fascination with the penis and vagina; the desire for sensual contact and stimulation of isolated body parts, orgiastic fantasies, and so on.

Few women will consciously have sexual intercourse with a man unless they feel some warmth, tenderness, and affection for him. Even the most blatantly promiscuous woman has difficulty admitting she fucked a man without any feeling for him as a person. The majority of men need no such excuse about their lack of Eros. Of all women only the whore can accept responsibility for the impersonal nature of her sexual relations with men. The "whorey" woman has therefore become an excellent and frequent symbol in the unconscious of many women for their own phallic sexuality.

How, then, can a woman come to a full conscious acceptance of her impersonal phallic sexuality and begin to take a responsible attitude toward it? Clearly she must first come to terms with the negative masculine Logos principle which dominates our culture. In order to do this, she needs to be able to explore her own thoughts, ideas, and images. But this is not possible until she is able to make a positive connection to a creative Logos principle, since feminine wisdom does not express itself in formulations.[3]

---

3. Ester Harding, *Woman's Mysteries*, New York: Pantheon, 1955, 232.

Where then can she find this helpful masculine spiritual guide so that she can formulate her own Feminine Mysteries? Even if she is able to find him, her experience with the masculine is going to make her very distrustful about following him. Fortunately, there seems to be inherent within the psyche of women such a guide, who takes the form of a truly positive animus or as an old wise man in her dreams. This fact can be readily substantiated by Jungian analysts all over the world and by their many women patients who have gone deeply enough into themselves.

It is, however, extremely difficult for a woman to maintain a positive connection to this internal guide or spiritual animus. Even in analysis, where a woman often experiences a male therapist as incarnating this understanding and supporting masculine principle, she is continually losing her positive connection. This is directly related to the incest wound. As I have indicated in other places, one of the manifestations of the incest wound is that the spiritual container for the integration of instinctual sexuality has been broken; instead of sexuality submitting to the service of Eros, it is repressed or it becomes rampant. In either case it interferes with the development of Eros. Unfortunately, as long as a woman is still involved in the therapeutic process with her analyst, a disruption of her positive connection to him tends to evoke a corresponding disturbance in her relationship to her own inner spiritual guide. This means that the process will be continually interrupted until instinctual sexuality finds its proper place in the relationship—the spiritual connection with the analyst always activates the unresolved incest problem.

We have now gone full circle and are back to the fundamental importance of a woman integrating her impersonal phallic sexuality if she is to serve Eros and remain true to her basic nature. The conundrum is this: she cannot integrate her impersonal sexuality until she has a connection to the creative masculine logos principle, but she cannot maintain this connection to Logos so long as she is guilty or rejecting of this aspect of her sexuality.

116

PHALLOS AND FEMININE PSYCHOLOGY

The effect of the incestuous triangle is to force the female child into an unconscious guilt-ridden relationship with her mother. Consequently, the archetypal mother principle that is forming within her psyche is experienced as a judgment and condemnation of her spontaneous instinctual urges, particularly sexuality; it does not matter if her actual mother is apparently accepting of her nature. The negative mother, therefore, is manifested as an inner voice which rejects and judges everything which is natural and instinctual in the woman. The conscious integration of instinctual sexuality cannot occur in a woman until she experiences a transformation of the Mother archetype. Then the positive mother brings Eros back into the woman's psyche as the ruling principle.

A woman with a severe negative mother problem found it impossible to allow herself to experience sexual memories of her childhood and adolescence. For many months whenever she came close to this area in her analysis, she was overwhelmed by anxiety to the point of panic. No amount of reassurance on my part seemed to help. Finally she had the following dream: "I was having an analytical hour with Dr. S. when his wife entered the room. She was a warm, motherly type of woman, and I liked her immediately. She stayed only a few minutes after asking her husband about some household matters."

This was an important dream. The appearance of an accepting maternal principle might finally free her to talk about her repressed sexuality and enable her to accept it emotionally. At her next visit this indeed proved to be the case; for the first time she was able to reveal to me the "dirty" and "sinful" sexuality of her past. More important than this, she was finally able to face this purulent material herself. After this she dreamt that a huge abcess of her big toe had been drained and that her toe had returned to normal. The phallic or Dactyl symbolism of the big toe is clear: it is as if her phallic sexuality had become hypertrophied and infected because of rejection and repression. This woman had been quite able to talk about adult sex, but not about those purely sensual, impersonal, sexual experiences from childhood and adolescence. Following this she had a dream in which a kindly

117

old professor of music told her she had a natural talent for the violin and that he was now ready to teach her. This professor is obviously an inner spiritual guide who will help her connect to her feelings and develop her eros function. Music is, of course, an excellent symbol for the expression of feelings and emotions. The symbolism of the violin probably places the emphasis on her need to learn to tune in and relate to others, as do the strings.

Since the relationship to the true father plays such an important role in determining a woman's adult pattern of relationship with men, let us briefly explore the nature of the father complex. A father fixation implies a serious lack of connection between the mother and father, and suggests that the father's anima was probably projected largely onto his daughter. The child tends to submit to this projection or resist it, although it is rare that it is purely one or the other. However one pattern is generally dominant, especially if the child has sisters. As I have indicated the incestuous triangle evokes guilt which usually results in a repression of erotic feelings toward father. However if the erotic aspect of the relationship is dominant, especially if there is actual sexual contact, then the spiritual kinship connection between father and daughter may slip into the unconscious, and the sexual nature of the relationship will be conscious. In either case a split between the spirit and the flesh occurs in such a relationship. Incest implies a total union of the opposites, mind and body; as long as one of these opposites is left out or split off, there will be little conscious guilt.

A woman with a father complex tends to fall into the same role with men as she had with her father, and the fragmenting effects of such a fixation make it difficult for a woman to bring her totality into a relationship with a man. Unfortunately as long as the archetypal masculine principle within her own soul remains unchanged, she will tend to continue in her habitual pattern all her life.

A deep analysis can effect remarkable changes in a woman's relationship to the inner masculine, the animus. However the task of establishing a positive connection often seems endless. She may come to a good relationship with one aspect of it only to find herself in a bad relationship with another, for the animus is split into many different forms which are continually in opposition to each other. Jung is empirically right when he describes the animus as multiple, though this is also a symptom of the split. If the woman experiences the animus often as a council of many judges, as Jung has suggested, it might be well to add that each member of this council has a different view as to what is right and wrong.

Although Jung has suggested that the anima is singular in a man, empirically the anima in modern man is also split, even if perhaps into not as many fragments as the animus. The major split in modern man's anima is between the spiritual and sensual aspects of the feminine principle: the Holy Mother Mary and the Goddess of erotic love, Aphrodite. A man cannot come to a positive connection to his anima until this split is reconciled and healed. The same is true of a woman in relationship to the animus. Although women in analysis tend to deal with each manifestation of the animus separately, they are continually undermined by this multiplicity of critical voices. Some familiarity with the various manifestations of the animus is essential, but until it is unified I believe the animus will continue to hound her and cut her off from her feminine nature.

The major division in the animus is identical to the anima: *spiritual and sensual.* The spiritual animus carries the following aspects of the Father principle: 1) the impulse to understand and to formulate the nature and meaning of man's existence; 2) an impulse to create form and order for the purpose of spiritual development and the continual humanization of man, e.g., it establishes the ethical and moral values of a culture, its ritual, laws, and the like; 3) a concern with love which is central to spiritual development, but which is largely expressed in creating forms for its humanization, such as marriage; 4) a respectful care for the dignity and freedom of the individual soul.

In addition the spiritual animus has other important functions which are best represented by the Brother and Son archetypes. The archetype of the Son is primarily a principle which fertilizes and

119

renews the Father, and consequently, the old cultural values. It is curious, explorative, imaginative, playful, daring, and explosive. It is an impulse toward spontaneous self-expression in contrast to the contemplative and conservative Father principle. The Brother archetype carries the eros-principle which desires spiritual intimacy and soul-connection with another. It is difficult to separate this archetype from its other half, the Sister. The Brother-Sister archetype, or the Incest archetype, is ultimately responsible for the soul connection between a man and a woman. A woman's connection to this aspect of her animus is therefore central; it makes it possible for her to experience her totality in a loving soul-to-soul meeting with a man. It is at once the archetype in Romantic Love and the Royal Marriage. The Brother-animus and Lover-animus are really one: the difference being that the taboo against incestuous union is lifted with the Lover. I have, of course, described only the positive manifestations of the spiritual animus.

It might be worth mentioning that the Father-Son archetypes are really two aspects of a totality; it would be more accurate to speak of the Father-Son archetype. The Brother animus is only one-half of the Brother-Sister archetype, which suggests that a woman's positive link to the masculine principle needs to be mediated through her positive connection to the Brother animus. The fact that Father, Son, and Brother all belong to a woman's kinship connections reveals the incestuous nature of a woman's connection to her spiritual animus. A woman suffering from guilt and fear as a result of unintegrated incestuous longings, will be unable to come to a positive connection with the spiritual animus until there has been considerable healing of her incest wound.

The sensual animus, on the other hand, contains the physical manifestations of phallic power and aggressiveness. It is *exogamous* and therefore holds the fear and fascination of the unknown other. Because it is not bound by the incest taboo, i.e., not realized as Father, Brother, Son, it offers the possibility of abandonment without fear of committing the terrible crime of incest. This sensual animus is the realm of the dark phallic gods—Priapus, Dionysus, Hades. It is Phallos which sets the flow of life in motion. It is impersonal, inhuman, and ruthless. It is the generative source of all human desires, from the highest to the lowest—lust, passion, exuberance, ecstasy. Without it we become cold, dry, and shrivelled. If a woman does not have a positive connection to this sensual aspect of the animus, neither can she have a *vital* relationship to the spiritual animus. One consequence of the incest wound is that a woman inhibits sexuality in relationship with the Brother animus; she can only be passionately aroused by the impersonal sensual animus.

Priapus demands obeisance and service from a woman. Aphrodite can be seen as his feminine counterpart; she must be served and worshipped by all men who desire the fruits of her love. It would seem that the spiritual animus, particularly the Father-Son Archetype, is there to serve and protect a woman, whereas Priapus, as the primal source of masculine power, demands her love, devotion, and service. One of the most frequent mistakes modern women seem to make in relationship to the animus is that they pour all their energy into serving or rebelling against the Father archetype while rejecting or profanely using Priapus.

It is not possible for a woman to come to a creative relationship with the spiritual animus if she does not have a worshipful and loving connection to Phallos, to the impersonal sensual powers within her own being. In an actual relationship with a man, devotion and service to Priapus will be manifest in her attitude and feeling towards the penis. The difficulty is that a woman needs the help of the spiritual animus to come to a positive connection and devotion to Phallos. Her connection to the spiritual animus must be mediated by the Brother-Sister archetype. This mediation is not possible if, like most modern women, she is suffering from the splitting effects of the incest wound. The healing of this wound and a positive connection to the Incest archetype must occur first. The healing of the incest wound involves, among other things, a gradually increasing awareness and acceptance of impersonal phallic sexuality within herself. This begins to open up a channel through which the gods of the upper and under world—Apollo and Dionysus—can eventually be united. But the union cannot occur until she is able to become a devoted servant and worshipper of Dionysus. Only then will Apollo, the spiritual animus, be able to give the care, protection, and spiritual strength to realize the needs of her individual soul.

When an archetype splits, one portion of it seems to function as a drive towards change and development—*Becoming*. Its opposite tends to manifest itself as a drive towards bodily survival and sensual pleasure—*Being*. Depending on which arm of the animus grips a woman, she will either be unmercifully driven to become something other than she is, or she will be compelled to reject all that nonsense about spiritual development and consciousness. She will be tossed back and forth between these opposites, criticized, and made to feel guilty and inadequate whenever she tries to be true to her feelings. In her actual relationships with men, she will be attracted alternately to a spiritual or a physical man, but she will feel inadequate as a woman with both, because at least one aspect of the animus will always be critical of her. Before she can become free of this constant harassment, this internal split of the masculine principle must be healed. Only then will she experience the animus as a non-judgmental, benevolent strength which protects the integrity of her *Being* and guides the process of her *Becoming*.

The critical voice of the animus may come from above or below. In actuality, it seems that the dark phallic gods give modem woman her worst time, because they have been most offended by her. They also know very well where to get to her. They make her feel dirty and inadequate, greedy, lascivious, sinful, or immoral about her own sexuality; they tell her that her sex stinks, that she is a whore, that she will never be a woman or make a man happy—besides, that all her ideas are stupid and foolish. These phallic gods also put the woman's intellect down and humiliate her much more than does the spiritual animus.

A woman in an acute psychotic state experienced masculine voices coming from above and below. Those from above took the position that she was intelligent and virtuous; those from below, which she experienced as diabolical little men or dwarfs, shouted obscenities at her day and night: "stupid whore," "filthy cunt," "fatherfucker," etc. This woman was, in fact, sexually indiscriminate when she had her first psychotic episode. In spite of this, she was unable to accept her own lust and sexual aggressiveness, projecting all the "dirty" sex onto men.

It is the full, *joyful* acceptance of the untamed and impersonal sexual thrust which the modern woman must experience before she is in any position to sacrifice it to a higher transforming power. A woman who has felt guilt and shame from early childhood about her instinctual sexuality needs, above all, to reconnect to this fertilizing, life-promoting aspect of her nature, to submit to it consciously in an emotional and impersonal experience. The attitude of the analyst toward this need can be crucial. Whether he has the Freudian tendency (to understand these persistent expressions for instinctual gratification as repressed infantile wishes which should not be acted out but rather made conscious and eventually sublimated), or if he has the Jungian tendency (to see them symbolically as expressions of the unconscious urge toward psychic wholeness), the woman continues to feel guilt about these dark impulses in her unredeemed nature. On the other hand, if the analyst can sacrifice his need for differentiation, and can recognize the necessity of instinctual energies expressed "as is," he constellates the maternal principle which accepts all that is natural. Otto Rank has put it very well: "an acceptance which means not merely a recognition or even admittance of our basic 'primitivity', in the sophisticated vein of our typical intellectuals, but a real allowance for its dynamic functioning in human behavior, which would not be lifelike without it."[4]

In ancient times, women were often required to have impersonal sexual experiences. For example Herodotus writes in his history:

> The worst Babylonian custom is that which compels every woman of the land once in her life to sit in the temple of Aphrodite and have intercourse with some stranger . . . the strangers pass and make their choice. After throwing a coin the man must say: "I demand thee in the name of the goddess Mylitta," for so the

---

4. Otto Rank, *Beyond Psychology*, New York: Dover Publications, 1958, 289.

Assyrians call Aphrodite. Whatever the value of the coin, she will not refuse it, for that would be unlawful, the coin being thought sacred. She goes with the first man who throws and rejects none. By having intercourse she has discharged her duty to the goddess and she goes away to her home: thereafter she is not to be won by any gift, however great . . . In some parts of Cyprus there is a custom of the same kind.[5]

The medieval custom in which the bride must spend the first night of her marriage with someone other than her husband, *jus primae noctus*, might be a variation of this ancient Babylonian custom.

Although our culture tacitly accepts the necessity for the freer expression of sexuality in women, there is no ritual whereby she can fully experience this without guilt and humiliation. Besides, it is not the freer expression of her phallic sexuality which a woman needs, but rather a sacred ritual whereby she can make an offering of this aspect of her sexuality to the goddess. She cannot truly serve the eros principle until she is released from the grip of her passions. In contrast to a sacred rite, the profane expressions of sexuality among modern women do not promote the transformation of eros which women need in order to maintain a loving relationship to a man (and to themselves).

A ritual such as we believe primitive and ancient woman had is certainly needed for modern woman. While this would make it more possible for her to relate positively and lovingly to a man, it leaves her still dependent on an actual man for her own completion. By offering the gift of her raw and undifferentiated phallic sexuality to the gods, she becomes more feminine, but she has also given up the source of her own phallic generative power. Therefore it is crucial to a woman's individuation that the return of this undifferentiated instinctual sexuality to consciousness should be in the form of *mental representations*. A woman will continually find herself caught between the opposing poles of her own masculine spirit until she learns to befriend and cultivate the sexual source of the masculine creative imagination.

---

5. Herodotus, *The Histories*, Vol. 1, New York: The Heritage Press, 1958, 82.

PHALLOS AND FEMININE PSYCHOLOGY

One aspect of a woman's animus—if she has gone no further in her psychological development than the sacrifice of her undifferentiated sexuality—will continue to make her feel guilty about the spontaneous thrusts of her being which have nothing to do with a relationship. This animus gets to her because he can make her feel cheap, unloving, and unfeminine whenever she attempts to follow the movements of her imagination. He can easily and rightly link any creative urge which is not directly involved with human relationships to dirty, unrelated, and undifferentiated sexuality; imaginative activity and inventiveness is after all a masculine prerogative, as is dirty sex. *Only if she can talk his language will she be able to deal adequately with his accusations.* In order to do this she has to be on the same familiar terms with her own impersonal phallic sexuality as he is. She must be as free of guilt as he is about allowing sexual imagery to enter consciousness. Once she can accept this type of mental sexuality as belonging to her nature, the attitude of the animus will also change. He will no longer demand that she always be open, related, and loving. He will begin to accept the fact that she can be imaginatively creative in areas other than the human relationship and still be womanly.

This whole question can be viewed from another perspective. Imaginative activity becomes obstructed if there are thoughts or images which are not allowed to enter consciousness. The early preoccupation of infants and children with the erotogenic zones and body imagery is now well established. The restrictions against immediate gratification of the sexual instinct which exist in all cultures—particularly the incest, menstruation, and masturbation taboos—tend to channelize some of the sexual libido into mental areas, thereby stimulating imaginative activity. It is these human sexual restrictions which are primarily responsible for humanity's uniquely creative mental processes. A woman can never realize her creative potential and her individuality if she allows only related sexuality to enter her consciousness.

PART FOUR

Eros

CHAPTER TEN

Eros and Thanatos

Originally Freud beleived that all instincts were in the service of Eros or the pleasure principle. But in 1920[1] he proposed a new dichotomy between Eros and the death instinct. The aim of Eros is to bind together, to establish ever-greater unities, and to preserve them. The aim of the death instinct is to undo connections and so to destroy things. He says, "We may suppose that the final aim of the destructive instinct is to reduce living things to an inorganic state."[2] His theory of a death instinct seems to be based largely on his assumption that the instincts are by nature conservative, and that "the state, whatever it may be, which a living thing has reached, gives rise to a tendency to re-establish that state so soon as it has been abandoned."[3] But of the Eros instinct he says, "We are unable to apply the formula to Eros" since its aim is to "establish ever greater unities."[4]

The starting point for these new reflections on the theory of instincts was Freud's need to understand more about the motives behind analytical resistance.[5] He observed that in the transference process, patients repeat all those unwanted situations and painful

---

1. Sigmund Freud, *Beyond the Pleasure Principle, Standard Edition,* XVIII, London: Hogarth Press, 1955.

2. Sigmund Freud, *An Outline of Psychoanalysis,* London: Hogarth Press, 1955, 6.

3. *Ibid.,* 5.

4. *Ibid.,* 6.

5. Sigmund Freud, *New Introductory Lectures on Psychoanalysis, Standard Edition,* XIII, London: Hogarth Press, 1964, 108.

emotions from the past. "They seek to bring about the interruptions of the treatment while it is still incomplete; they contrive once more to feel themselves scorned, to oblige the physician to speak severly to them and treat them coldly; they discover appropriate objects for their jealousy . . . . None of these things can have produced pleasure in the past, and might be supposed that they would cause less unpleasure today if they emerged as memories or dreams instead of taking the form of fresh experiences."[6] Based upon behavior in the transference and upon life-histories of men and women, Freud concluded, "that there really does exist in the mind a compulsion to repeat which overrides the pleasure principle."[7]

Freud felt it was self-destructive for the patient to resist the efforts of the analyst's attempts to help him. Jung has given sufficient evidence to show that this is not neccesarily the case, that analytic resistance frequently comes from healthy self-protective instincts.[8] My own investigations into this area have led me to conclude that the fundamental need of the soul in any relationship is the desire for union with the other person. Resistance develops primarily as a result of the frustrations centering around this need. True communion is not possible without mutual exposure. This means that no aspect of one's soul can be rejected, that the totality of one's being must be fully embraced. The analytical situation constellates this need for exposure, but the patient continues to resist until realizing that the analyst is not only willing but desirous of similar exposure. If the analyst does not recognize and accept the need for communion, it is self-destructive for the patient to expose the soul to the fragmenting distortions of the objective observer. The true nature of the soul can only be revealed in communion. I believe that therapeutic resistance, particularly in psychoanalysis, comes largely from the insistence that an analyst maintain an objective stance.

---

6. Freud, *Beyond the Pleasure Principle*, 43.

7. *Ibid.*, 46

8. C. G. Jung, "Fundamental Questions of Psychotherapy," *CW 16*, New York: Pantheon, 1954, §237

EROS AND THANATOS

Still we are left with the need to explain the self-destructive tendencies so obvious in many people, the compulsion to repeat destructive patterns of behavior. In my experience individuals having an impaired capacity to form close relationships are most likely to be plagued with persistent self-destructive behavior patterns; this suggests that there is a relationship between these tendencies and a disturbance in the development of the Eros function. Since Eros development and the humanization of the animal instincts go hand in hand, self-destructiveness is frequently a manifestation of damaged instincts. The idea that our neglected and abused animal natures can turn against us, seems a much more meaningful and accurate explanation for self destructiveness than the death instinct theory.

There is yet another criticism of Freud's assumption that the final aim of the destructive instinct is to reduce living things to an inorganic state. This view comes from a materialistic bias, which postulates a somatic origin of the human psyche. The idea that the human spirit is primary and antecedent to the soma, that it is both the activating and formative principle, leads to different conclusions. Instead of conceiving the life principle, mechanistically, as originating out of inorganic matter and ultimately returning to this original state, the goal of human life is seen rather as an unfolding and original incarnation of a spiritual principle. Death is an indication that the spirit or soul has acheived the best possible expression of its creative urge in that particular body. Death is not the destuction of this creation and the return to an inorganic state. What is buried in the earth is not true soul, but the husk, the shell which has gradually assumed the same shape and form as soul. Death is but the shedding of the old skin so that the soul can be freed to reincarnate itself in a new creation.

CHAPTER ELEVEN

The Transformation of Eros

I

Modern theories about instinct offer no adequate explanation for humanity's capacity to endure conflict for the specific purpose of spiritual or psychological development. There is not the slightest evidence that animals have anything like the human ability to endure pain and suffering, to restrain from pleasurable gratification. The sudden inhibition or redirection of instinctual discharge does exist in animals, but this is hardly a matter of freedom of choice as it can be in a human. The capacity to choose between instinctual discharge and restraint or inhibition is, as far as I know, characteristic only of humans.

Another fundamental weakness in Freud's theory of instincts is his view of what he has termed the Eros instincts. For example he states that these instincts are under the rule of the pleasure principle. This is not necessarily consistent with his other statement that the aim of Eros is "to bind together, to establish ever greater unites." Here he is really talking about a creative process or principle which moves toward a unification of the opposites in order to form an original whole. The instincts under the rule of the pleasure principle are basically not concerned with union but with pleasurable discharge and the avoidance of pain.

Human psychological development demands, among other things, the restraint of instinctual gratification and the capacity to endure displeasure. Under the rule of the pleasure principle, the instincts contain no inherent characteristic sufficient to explain the persistent human need for creative psychological development. The Freudian view that they are redirected or sublimated by the external restrictions of culture always leaves one vital question unanswered: *What is the impulse or* instinct *behind the human need to form cultures which impose restrictions on animal-sensual gratification?* Would it not be more meaningful to postulate an uniquely human instinct designed to promote the creative evolution of the human psyche? Jung has proposed an instinct toward individuation, a religious or spiritual instinct, and in at least one place he has called it the creative instinct.[1]

Since Eros has always been associated with human love and human intercourse, it is unfortunate that Freud chose this term to refer to the undifferentiated sexual energies under the rule of the pleasure principle. The desire for something more than instinctual discharge and sensual gratification in the human relationship is a function of the creative principle of union. In human relationships at least, we must assume an identity between the Creative instinct and Eros. This different usage of the term Eros, in many ways a polar opposite to the pleasure principle, is of course confusing. Perhaps it would be best to drop the term, but I believe Eros needs to be restored to its rightful place as the function of creative human intercourse.

A more comprehensive theory of the dynamics of the human soul demands that we hypothesize at least an additional instinct to explain humanity's unique characteristics. The inclusion of a creative or spiritual instinct would seem to be essential for any human instinct theory. In addition such a formulation establishes a necessary link to the ancient idea of the human soul as consisting of an unique spiritual portion as well as an animal-sensual portion.

The understanding and ultimate resolution of the mind/body split in modern people necessitates a thorough exploration of the relationship and interaction between the sensual and spiritual aspects of the soul. I have already suggested that the nature of the spiritual or creative

---

1. C. G. Jung, "Psychological Factors in Human Behavior," *CW 8*, New York: Pantheon, 1960, § 245.

instinct is similar, if not identical, to the nature of Eros.[2] With this formulation, Eros or the Creative Principle, would form one portion of the soul, and the Basic Instincts under the rule of the Pleasure Principle, would form the other.

The assumption that Eros and the Creative Instinct are identical is based upon still another assumption: that creativity is a function of the principle of union through which the opposites unite to create new wholes. Eros and the Creative Instinct meet in this urge or movement toward union. The essence of creativity, whether it manifests itself in human relationships and development or in creative works, is love.

The experience of love initially is toward a person or object outside of oneself. Creative works emerge out of a relationship with internal images, thoughts, ideas, sensations, and feelings; in other words, out of an internal connection and union. Still it is the principle of union—love—as an internal function and experience which is necessary for creative activity. Therefore the development of the love function is of supreme importance for creative action and living. The imaginative activity of a child and its expression in play, for example, is generally blocked when there is a serious disturbance in the child's positive connection to others.

Even according to Freud's theory of psychosexual development, sexuality expresses itself as a drive toward sensual gratification and discharge rather than as an urge toward union, at least until the stage of genital sexuality is achieved. Only through a gradual process of transformation do the basic instinctual drives begin to function toward the creation of new wholes and greater unities. Untouched by the transforming power of Eros, there is no possibility for the humanization of these instincts. Were people ruled by the pleasure-principle instead of the creative-principle, our unique psychological and cultural development would never have occurred.

A child lives under the reign of the pleasure-principle. Gradually, with the help of education, discipline and ritual, the creative instinct

---

2. See James Hillman, "On Psychological Creativity," *The Myth of Analysis*, Evanston, Ill.: Northwestern UP, 1972, for an oustanding discussion on this view.

emerges to challenge the supremacy of the pleasure-principle. It manifests itself initially in the child's growing awareness of and concern with the effect of its spontaneous expressions on others. The creative first reveals itself in the child's psyche as that archetypal force concerned with relationship. This idea becomes more meaningful if we understand the idea of relationship with another to be a movement toward union or communion. While the pleasure-principle always expresses itself as an urge toward discharge and gratification, the creative principle always manifests itself as a desire to produce an original form. *The union of the opposites, out of which an unknown and mysterious third is born, is the essence of the creative.* It is this transforming quality of the human soul which, in addition to forming, shaping, and continually changing the world, continually transforms and changes humanity. Eros development, therefore, is not so much determined by the degree of basic instinctual expression and gratification permitted by a culture (as Marcuse seems to believe),[3] but by the viability of those social forms and rituals which are designed to promote the development of the creative instinct.

Creativity, in our Western culture at least, has been largely identified with creative works. The human relationship and its effects on the individual have been viewed essentially as a natural expression, development, and modification of basic instinctual drives. Reason and consciousness, if anything, are proclaimed as humanity's special gifts, which account for our unique position in the evolutionary scale as the only truly creative creature. Love, the essential ingredient for the human connection, is not considered an uniquely human attribute, neither by scientists nor theologians. Reason and consciousness are *sui generis* considered to be able to develop, expand, and transform. Love, on the other hand, like sex and hunger, is conceived as an essentially blind and undifferentiated drive which can only be altered if it comes in contact with rational consciousness. As everyone knows the rational mind is not a particularly reliable guide in human

---

3. Herbert Maarcuse, *Eros and Civilization*, New York: Vintage Books, 1962.

relationships. It has little effect in promoting intimacy and connection with another; if anything it has come to function more often as an obstruction. If reason and consciousness are identified as *the* creative instruments given to people, it is small wonder that the essentially irrational nature of the human connection has been overlooked as the *opus magnum* of the creative instinct.

Love is primarily a movement toward union. Perhaps love is *the* principle of union. As such it is identical to the creative-principle. Here we come to the heart of the matter. *If love and the creative urge are one and the same thing, then the human connection is obviously central to creativity.* However love can no longer be thought to be blind for it must be capable of direction and vision.[4] In addition it must be capable of transforming itself as well as being transforming. It is my conviction that humanity is continually being created as a result of the transformation which the creative instinct (Love) undergoes.

Love, that great movement toward union, is the transforming principle, the creative instinct, which itself transforms in the process of transforming. Love flows outward to join one's soul with another, and it flows internally to promote wholeness by uniting mind and body, humanity's spiritual and animal natures. But the love connection to another soul is primary, both as an initiating and sustaining force for inner union and wholeness. This would correspond to Buber's statement that, "you cannot really love God if you do not love men . . ." And to his disagreement with Kierkegaard's view that one shall have to do essentially only with God. Buber counters this statement with the Hasidic view that, "One cannot have to do essentially with God if one does not have to do essentially with men."[5]

---

4. Rollo May, in his excellent work, *Love and Will*, New York: W. W. Norton & Co., 1969, makes important contributions to our understanding of the function of Eros in Human development. He lends support to many of my views, including the idea that Eros has direction and purpose.

5. Martin Buber, "Love of God and Love of Neighbor," *Hasidism and Modern Man*, New York: Harper Torchbooks, 1958, 283.

II

The soul is not basically in opposition to the body. It contains the instincts responsible for the health and survival of the body as well as the creative urge toward continual transformation through union. The care of the body (Being) is largely regulated by the instinctual urge toward sensual gratification and the avoidance of pain, but the developmental movement toward creative unfolding (Becoming) is ruled and regulated by love. In a child, as in an animal, the soul is whole because the love instinct, with its care and concern for others, only emerges gradually. There is no conflict between the need for immediate sensual gratification and love. However as soon as the child begins to care about its effect on others, the soul is thrown into conflict which tends to split it. It is at this point that the mind/body split often occurs—but it need not happen; the conflict, yes, but the resolution of this conflict is contained within the creative instinct, love. In other words love can unite the drive for immediate sensual gratification with the urge toward a creative becoming. For the child it is crucial that the forms, rituals, and structure of society should be designed to promote this union. Otherwise the sensual/spiritual split in his soul is inevitable.

This conflict between the spirit and the flesh, between creative becoming and sensual being, and its resolution through union, contains the essence of humanity's creative transformation. Through this process humanity's soul continually renews and transforms itself. It is never resolved once and for all, and its form also continually changes. Always it is love which brings about its resolution. However, as I have indicated, love itself is continually transforming, so that the love which unifies the soul conflict in a child is qualitatively different than the love of an adult.

The idea that love transforms itself follows from this basic premise concerning the nature and substance of the soul. That is the soul contains essentially one portion which is love and desires only to create through love, and another portion which is instinctual sensuality, desiring only immediate gratification and the avoidance of pain. The conflict between the spiritual and sensual aspects of the soul and its repeated resolution through union is the nature of the process through which each soul realizes and fulfills its unique destiny. Each time this union occurs, both aspects of the soul are also transformed. The love portion is no longer the same after true union, nor is the instinctual-sensual portion.

Further insight into the nature of this phenomenon can perhaps best be gathered by examining the experience of the analytical relationship. Both Freud and Jung have indicated that the sublimation or transformation of the instincts is an important goal of analysis, so we should be able to give evidence of a fundamental change occurring in the sensual portion of the soul. However the idea that love transforms has been neglected in analytical thought, as far as I know, even though its transforming effects are well recognized. If my view is correct, then any transformation of our instinctual nature would have to be accompanied by a fundamental change in our love nature. Conversely, if there is no evidence of change in our love nature, it should make us suspicious of any superficial evidence which might suggest a change in our animal-sensual nature.

Love and the need for instinctual discharge and gratification can clearly oppose each other, but this is only true during the state of conflict, where love acts as a restraining force. However they are not in opposition, because love aims for sensual gratification as well as spiritual fulfillment. The flow of love is, in fact, always experienced through the blood stream. It is an intensely warm and pleasurable sensual experience, more pleasurable, qualitatively and quantitatively, than instinctual discharge. Nevertheless the need for sensual gratification, apart from love, must never be devalued just because love seems to offer so much more. Love also functions to create a balance and harmony between the process of Being and Becoming. It can be destructive to the health of the body for a person to endure too much sensual deprivation while waiting with all the Christian virtues of humility, dedication, and perserverance, for love to resolve the conflict. In fact the animal-sensual portion of the soul needs to be treated with the same loving care and understanding as does the creative-spiritual portion, otherwise it turns against us and obstructs union. Often submission to sensuality is needed in order to release the stream of love. Such a submission can be the very act of love which, by its absence, has prevented the opposites from uniting.

I have, in effect, been describing another area of conflict which is created by love. It is the other side of love's command to endure the conflict of the opposites. Perhaps it can best be described as love's limitation on limitation. It would appear that though love is a great flow toward union, it is also the great restraining and regulating instrument of the human soul. Compared to love the rational mind is a most inadequate instrument for regulating the ebb and flow of vital human energies. It is far too gross and general, lacking the sensitive sympathetic connection to the subtle movements of the soul in the living body.

Love, then, is both the Creator and the Directing Intelligence within the soul of humanity. But it is also a continually changing intelligence which is sensitively in tune with the living moment. Its commands are never fixed and rigid. While it may demand restraint of sensual gratification at one moment, in the next it may desire submission to sensuality. It is far different than the Logos of the Old Testament God. Nevertheless it also contains a Logos principle through its function of restraint and limitation.[6] This regulatory function of love is, as I have indicated, not at all the blind force which Western culture has come to identify it with. Untransformed love, in its primal, undifferentiated state, does appear as a blind force. But contained within the archetype of love is the restraining and regulating intelligence which, under satisfactory cultural conditions, leads ultimately to its own transformation. Love must be gradually humanized before it can be trusted to protect both the health and survival of the body as well as its creative unfolding. Until love has been sufficiently

---

6. See the discussion of Eros/Logos in Chapter Eight, 162f.

humanized, it needs to be subjected to outer forms of regulation which have proven effective in promoting its development and transformation.

III

What or who is Eros? Is Eros identical with love? Is it the principle of psychic relatedness, as Jung has suggested? Is it masculine or feminine? The evidence seems to point to its masculine nature and representation in both Western and Eastern tradition. When Eros is conceived as feminine, the principle of openness, receptivity and responsiveness is stressed. As a masculine Deity it becomes a much more active, outgoing, penetrating, and, therefore, phallic principle. Eros is at once the *great opener* and the *great receiver—so* that its true nature is hermaphroditic. Still, it reveals itself most clearly in its active, outflowing manifestations, which explains its predominately masculine representations.

Above all Eros seems to function as a mediator between the Divine and human.[7] If it were not for Eros, people would have little say or choice about life. Only through Eros, as intermediary, can a person establish an individual relationship with the Divine. Eros enables people to restrain, to say nay to the numinous influx of the Gods without breaking the communion. In contrast the rational mind is overwhelmed when a divine power like Love enters the soul. Without Eros the rational mind is either obliterated by direct encounter with the Divine, or it must detach itself from the body and block out all sensations and feelings.

Eros, as the intermediary function, must itself transform as a human soul evolves. Thus it is possible to speak of a childhood of Eros. In its undeveloped state it is essentially a yea-sayer, surrendering to the Divine command without question. Only as it matures does it begin to become a reliable guide regulating the ebb and flow of the Powers which give life and meaning to one's existence. Where there have been damaging developmental experiences, an individual tends

---

7. Plato, *Symposium*, 203 A. For further discussion of Eros as a figure of the metaxy, the intermediate region, see Hillman, *op. cit.*

to use the rational mind as the directing intelligence; otherwise, one lives unconsciously, completely at the mercy of the primal life forces.

The idea that God or the Gods change seems questionable. Are not the eternal, unchanging, natural forces manifestations of the Gods? Are the cosmic forces any less awesome, any more human, than they ever were? I think not. Only humanity's relationship to the Gods changes.[8] Any appearance of change in the Diety is delusion, a direct result of humanity's changing attitudes and relationship to It. Love is a God or a Goddess. As such it is an eternal, unchanging elemental force. Each time man is moved by this Great Power, it must enter his soul freshly and be humanly shaped by Eros.

Love is the matrix out of which Eros is born and emerges, just as the Greek Eros is the son of the Goddess of Love. Hence love is primary. If we understand love to be simply that enormous life force which moves us toward union and fusion with another, we will be describing a vital aspect of the nature of Eros. If in addition we understand love as being responsible for our adoration and devotion to another, this also describes Eros. But love without Eros is notoriously fickle and promiscuous. Love is not the substance which binds two people together permanently. It is a free spirit which cannot be committed to the particular and unique, because it must move toward union with all of life. Love is no more able than reason to take care of a human relationship. Without Eros love is as impersonal and ultimately as destructive to the human connection as is Logos without Eros. Eros, then, must be understood as the guardian and protector of human love and connection. A fundamental difference between the two is that Eros desires a creative development of a particular relationship more than it desires union. Love is the basic ingredient. But Eros is the transforming vessel.

Active Eros moves always toward connection and union with the soul of the other. Here is where it might appear to be identical with love, except it does not always express itself so lovingly. Active Eros

---

8. Cf. Jung's view on this issue in "Answer to Job," *CW 11*, New York: Pantheon, 1958.

is free to express itself through the range of human emotions and reactions but always as a unique and spontaneous response to the other and out of a desire for closeness. It demands that we overcome the fear of hurting the other, that we trust the spontaneous expression and reactions of our own being in relationship to the other. Active Eros is obstructed if one person feels burdened with the responsibility of protecting another from the potential or possible hurts which one's spontaneous reaction may inflict. In the analytical relationship, for example, the burden of therapeutic responsibility can be obstructive to Eros. Before Eros can be totally free to express itself, there must be a feeling of equality, and one person must not feel responsible for the welfare of the other.

We have been discussing Eros in its active, outflowing, and giving manifestations, but there is equally an inherent strong countermovement. The protective function of Eros is contained in this diastolic wave which is experienced as a restraining or inhibiting force. Unfortunately this withdrawal and closing off of the flow of Eros is generally experienced as a negative or bad thing; instead of having respect and gratitude for this regulating action of Eros, we make desperate attempts to overcome it. Socrates, for example, recognized that his personal daimon was Eros, and he was particularly attentive to its inhibiting action. Therefore he trusted his decision to take the lethal hemlock because his daimon (Eros) gave absolutely no indication of opposition.[9]

Eros has no need to express itself in violent action. Only when we fail to listen to its rhythmical ebb and flow does it descend upon us with its sword. D. H. Lawrence, in his description of Sir Clifford's reaction upon being informed of Connie's relationship with Mellors, gives us a penetrating glimpse into one of the consequences of the failure to pay heed to the warning voice of Eros:

---

9. Plato, *Apology*, 40 D.

Clifford was not *inwardly* surprised to get this letter. Inwardly, he had known for a long time she was leaving him. But he absolutely refused any outward admission of it. Therefore, outwardly, it came as the most terrible blow and shock to him . . .

And that is how we are. By strength of will we cut off our inner intuitive knowledge from admitted consciousness. This causes a state of dread, or apprehension, which makes the blow ten times worse when it does fall.[10]

A bad relationship to the restraining function of Eros manifests itself most vividly and immediately in our sexual relationships. If we listen respectfully to our guilts and fears, our anxieties, our lack or loss of desire, our impotencies and failures to achieve orgasm, the connection will not be broken. A woman, for example, who has a firm connection to her own Eros, will not feel inadequate, resentful, or blameful toward her husband when she finds herself unresponsive to his sexual advances. In the plainest language Eros is telling her that a physical union is not possible at the moment.

You say, "Of course, how terribly obvious, tell us something we don't know!" Well, why not add, "He doesn't really want me, he has no connection to me personally. He only wants to satisfy his sexual urge. If he really wanted me, I would respond." And why not let out all of your years of resentment toward him for his lack of feeling and respect for you, for his lack of real passion, his unrelated and impersonal masturbatory sex? And why not, for good measure, throw in the generally accepted fact that men primarily want sex from a woman and care little about relationship? But *this is* not what Eros was trying to say when it restrained and inhibited you. Eros is never critical or resentful about the impersonal phallic thrust, even though it may retreat from it. Although Eros desires to effect a union between two individual souls, it is not destroyed by the impersonal forces which make such a union impossible. Eros never loses touch with its desire for union with

10. D. H. Lawrence, *Lady Chatterley's Lover*, New York: Grove Press, 1959, 348.

the other; even while it may retreat from the sting of the dehumanizing thrust of the impersonal, it still embraces it even as it restrains. In this restraining embrace Eros expresses its warm-blooded, human, and personal reaction to the other. This has an immediate, humanizing effect on the impersonal archetype or instinct which threatens to break the connection.

A woman who was threatened by her husband's impersonal Logos and repelled by his sexual advances, had this dream:

> I was in a room and a threatening monstrous man was coming toward me. My grandmother was in the background and she kept warning me to run and hide or hit him with an iron poker. As he came closer, he reminded me a bit of my husband. I suddenly reached out and took his hands and we began to dance around the room with our arms upraised. I was afraid but became less so as we danced He seemed to soften somewhat. My grandmother kept shouting for me to kill him, but I tried not to listen to her. Gradually I began to lose my fear and he seemed to become more human as I looked into his eyes. I was no longer repelled or frightened of him. In fact, I was about to kiss him as I awakened.

This idea of the "restraining embrace" best describes how Eros functions to protect a person against the potential destructiveness of impersonal archetypal and instinctual forces.

IV

Without the human connection the transformation of the basic instincts and their internalization through the process of a continual and evolving union with Eros cannot occur. Gradually the physical-sensual appetites change and lose some of their demonic compulsiveness. The creative instinct also has a demonic quality, and it, too, must be and is humanized through its unfolding union with the animal-sensual portion of the soul, or to put it differently, through the evolving process of incarnation in the lower centers of body consciousness.

145

ROBERT STEIN

For example erotic love is one of the most powerful experiences a person can have. In its untransformed state it combines all the compulsiveness of the sensual appetites and the demonic urge toward creativity. The destructive potentialities of the creative urge are well known. But erotic love is so overwhelmingly compulsive and demonic not only because it is an expression of sexual lust and passion but because it is combined with a primal expression of the creative instinct.

When the powerful emotions of erotic love take over, we see little of the restraining function of Eros. Thus when two people surrender to pure eroticism, without giving sufficient time to the care of the relationship, the pleasure-principle may be gratified, but the human connection does not have a chance to develop. Primitive Eros, like primitive sexuality, must transform if it is to function creatively.

If the restraining function in primitive Eros is undeveloped, Eros is no more to be trusted as a guide than is the sexual instinct. How then is the development of Eros promoted so that it can function as the transforming principle it really is? One thing seems to be necessary: the knowledge through experience of how destructive unrestrained surrender to erotic love can be. After an individual has enough of these experiences, perhaps Eros may begin to manifest some restraint. However I think if we look at some of the cultural factors which enter into the humanization of a child, especially in a reasonably healthy society, we will be more likely to find our answer. It seems to be necessary for the development of a child that limits and restraints should be imposed from without. The same is true, in my opinion, for the "childhood of Eros."

As long as Eros is still the mighty demon unable to say "no" to Aphrodite, outer restraint is necessary. The same holds true for the sensual instincts until Eros is humanized. Thus a child needs cultural and parental restraint until its basic instincts and the creative instinct have undergone sufficient transformation. Until the restraining function of Eros is experienced as a positive internal creative force, instead of externally as a protective or oppressive strength belonging to parental figures, the child is not ready to assume responsibility for the care of

146

its own soul. Only after Eros is firmly internalized and experienced as a reliable instrument for regulating the soul's activities, does a *sustained* and truly creative relationship become possible.

V

Analysis reveals the wounds of love. These wounds can be described as experiences of betrayal by and disillusionment with Eros, beginning with the original wounding experiences with one's parents. Hence the patient feels that Eros is not to be trusted. Analysis must be able to redeem Eros and reestablish the analysand's connection and trust in it. All the good work and development in an analysis can be obliterated if the analysand once again experiences a betrayal by Eros. Eros never betrays when it is internalized, a state which can only occur when it is humanized. Thus we only experience love as a betrayer when we are dependent on another person to keep us connected to it. Your love will never betray me if I have a firm connection with my own love, because my love will take care of me. One who is betrayed by those one loves, does not know Eros.

What is the nature of the forms and rituals people need in order to ensure the transformation of erotic love into a creative relationship? If we are able to grasp the pattern and myth of this process, it may lead us toward a more complete psychotherapeutic model and new cultural models for promoting Eros development. Let us first examine childhood. The intense and driving passion of erotic love cannot be experienced in a child until it has reached sexual maturity. A child lives largely under the rule of the pleasure-principle, the need for sensual release and gratification, but this is not the same thing as erotic love. In a child pure instinctual sexuality does not become firmly fixed to one person or object. It can be pleasurably discharged in many different ways. Eros, on the other hand, becomes firmly fixed to one person or object. When coupled with instinctual sensuality, as it is in erotic love, it cannot really be fulfilled except in relationship to the object of its love.

Even though the pleasure-principle dominates the life of childhood, the emotion of love begins to emerge and slowly develop early. However love does not have the same power or compulsive demand on the child as does its instinctual sensual nature. Only with the experience of erotic love is the demonic power of the creative instinct first revealed. Perhaps it is also the first experience of the essential unity of the two great powers responsible for the life, health, and development of a person's physical and spiritual nature.

Before the experience of erotic love can occur, two things must happen: the sexual nature of the child needs to be sufficiently developed, and an awareness of the need for spiritual intimacy to another must have formed within the child's psyche. This does not occur automatically, and it will not occur if there has been a serious disturbance of the child's sexual development and a feeling connection to others, which go hand in hand. It is not too unusual, nowadays, to encounter adults who have never experienced the intense passion and consuming desire of erotic love, which surely indicates a serious disturbance in psychosexual development. We must examine some of the factors necessary to the experience of erotic love before we can understand the process of its transformation into a creative relationship. I suspect that both processes are interrelated.

The healthy sexual development of a child is dependent primarily on the existence of adequate external regulation. However the outer limitations must allow for sufficient expression and discharge of the instincts. The success of this delicate balance between the spontaneous expression of instinctual needs and restraint depends on the state of development of the cultural Eros. Hand in hand with the regulation of instinctual discharge, the cultural Eros must create forms and rites which promote the sanctification of the living body and the mystery of the human connection. This means that the archetype of union, the Heavenly Marriage, needs to be experienced by the child in its incarnation in the human marriage. The rites and regulations surrounding the incest taboo largely determine the direction which this fundamental experience of the Eros principle will take.

THE TRANSFORMATION OF EROS

Thus a child is psychologically prepared to open up to the intense passion of erotic love only if it has experienced the need for spiritual intimacy with another, and if it has been able to freely explore the vicissitudes of his sexual instinct. This also implies that a certain amount of psychisation and internalization of Eros has already occurred, but it is far from the stable form needed to support a prolonged creative relationship. In erotic love the power of Eros is first experienced in its demonic and still insufficiently humanized form. However the capacity to experience erotic love indicates that a considerable amount of internalization has already occurred. The soul is now ready to participate in the crucial transformation of Eros into the creative human function.

The way is prepared for the full internalization of Eros once the soul is able to endure the heat and passion of erotic love. Our culture has failed to supply the forms and rituals essential for such Eros development, and many people have turned to analysis hoping to heal the wounds caused by this failure. I will attempt to describe the nature of this healing process as I have seen it shaping itself in the analytical ritual.

But let us first briefly review the requirements of a sound Eros-oriented culture. Fundamentally it must make it possible for the child to totally accept its instinctual life as it emerges into consciousness, without the necessity of guilt and repression. The social forms, rituals, and mores of such a culture must contain room for spontaneous expression of instinctual needs and defined restraints and limitations. This promotes the transformation of the basic sensual instincts and Eros, thereby creating the right conditions for developing the child's capacity to enter into creative human connections. *It has to be a non-repressive culture.*

CHAPTER TWELVE
Eros and The Analytical Ritual

The psychoanalytic ritual is above all designed to create an antirepressive therapeutic environment (whether or not it achieves this goal we shall see later). The foundation of the analytical model is the creation of a form which allows a patient complete freedom to express verbally all the neglected, repressed, defamed, and guilt-ridden thoughts, feelings, and emotions. Along with the freedom, definite and strict limitations were early introduced by Freud. They can be summarized as follows:

1) *A taboo against the analyst's emotional involvement*—the patient must accept that the analyst's personal and spontaneous reactions will be withheld, and that the analyst will function primarily as an objective, but sympathetic observer who offers the patient the benefits of rational knowledge and understanding.

2) *A taboo against physical-sensual expression*—the patient must agree to limit the expression of being to verbal forms or physical gestures which do not involve physical contact with the analyst.

3) *Time and place*—the patient must agree to meet with the analyst only within the restrictions of the consulting room and for a specified length of time and frequency.

4) *Money*—the patient must agree to pay a specified amount of money and to assume responsibility for its prompt payment.

This model would seem to incorporate the type of non-repressive freedom and restraint which I have suggested is essential for an Eros

151

oriented culture. We will not, at the moment, question the adequacy of this form, since we are attempting to establish the nature of the archetypal pattern.

The fact that the human relationship is the *sine qua non* for psychological development forced Freud to the realization that the so-called transference phenomenon was the alpha and omega of psychoanalysis. Human relationship, expressed as transference and countertransference, thus became the central focus of his opus. However, it is certainly a strange distortion of the human connection when there is a demand that one party maintain an objective distance from any personal or emotional involvement, while the other is encouraged and expected to become completely involved and entangled emotionally. This can hardly be called human. It has no historical precedent, so far as I know, except as a manifestation or incarnation of the disturbed and distorted parent-child or teacher-pupil relationship. Perhaps it is just this impossibility of experiencing a truly human communion which constellates the therapeutic goal: namely, the emotional experience and the realization of the vicissitudes of the soul's negative and futile struggle to establish a human connection. Through these emotional and mental experiences, a certain amount of energy is released and made available to the ego. This energy, when it is combined with increased knowledge of the destructive unconscious forces that interfere with human relationships, *increases the ego's strength and capacity to control and regulate the direction of the instinctual-emotional life.* That is, if the ego orientation of the psychoanalytical *Weltanschaaung is* accepted.

This attempt to describe the structure of the psychoanalytic model does it an injustice because of the brevity, but I believe it is accurate enough for our purpose. It shows that the creative regulation of the instinctual-emotional life, especially in human relationships, is the goal, and that this goal is achieved with the working through of the relationship between analyst and patient. Thus the goal and the way center around the human relationship. The structure is designed to create the possibility for considerable freedom of expression (for the analysand), combined with clearly defined limitations. The question is, does psychoanalysis achieve its goal with this model? Can it? Also is this goal identical to our goal of the psychologically creative relationship through the internalization of Eros?

I have suggested that the experience of erotic love is perhaps one's first experience with the relationship of the union of one's sensual and creative nature: a simultaneous expression of internal union and of a movement toward union with another. For this reason it is perhaps a root metaphor for a creative relationship. The frequency of erotic transferences among women patients led the genius of Freud to the realization that this was somehow central to the process. The psychoanalytical ritual, for women at least, became largely a matter of the woman's struggle with the vicissitudes of her frustrated and ambivalent feelings toward the analyst. It is perhaps not accurate to take erotic love as the model for the creative relationship, unless both parties are gripped by this powerful urge toward physical and spiritual union. In which case the model of "falling in love" or "being in love" would more accurately describe the condition. Since it is only the patient who is allowed to fall in love with the analyst, it is the potential for a truly human connection which is constellated in the psychoanalytical situation rather than its realization.

Since it lacks the possibility for a mutual psychologically creative relationship, the goal of psychoanalysis is clearly not identical to our goal. But we must still see whether it achieves a creative regulation of the instinctual-emotional life, especially in the human relationship. I suppose our answer depends largely on our concept of "creative regulation." The philosophical and metaphysical orientation of psychoanalysis places ego consciousness (or the rational mind) in the center of its regulatory system. The educational experience of psychoanalysis enlarges ego-consciousness, thereby enabling the ego to allow a much wider range of feelings and emotions to enter its field of awareness, without having to fall back on the protective mechanism of repression. Psychoanalysis makes its greatest contribution toward increasing the ego's capacity to deal with the repressed instinctual-emotional life by replacing the repressive, guilt-producing Judeo-Christian concept of sin with a new liberating concept: one's "evil" thoughts and desires are no longer experienced as a sin in the Eye of God. The psychoanalytic *Weltanschaaung* has turned the Biblical concept of sin into a virtue. To be able to think, feel, and verbally express the most negative and evil aspects of one's being is the path to health and happiness. To allow the repressed to return to consciousness is good; to turn away from the temptation of evil is bad. Evil belongs in the rational mind, where it can be elevated from its emotional-bodily roots and become a mental phenomenon. But to respond directly to one's animal-sensual nature, to "act out," is as much a Freudian sin as it is a Judeo-Christian transgression. In other words the regulation of the instinctual-emotional life is achieved through its transformation into mental constructs and images. Now if I desire my neighbor's wife, I no longer need to repress it and suffer from paralyzing neurotic guilt. I can think about my desires all I want, and possibly even turn them into some creative work. My ego has discovered a way of controlling and regulating the sensual demands of the pleasure-principle. It has attained that same level of detachment and objectivity which my analyst effectively demonstrated to me. It is now in a position to contain and withhold any of the spontaneous expressions of my being which might involve and entangle me irrationally and "unreasonably" with another human being. I no longer need to fear that my ego may be dethroned by the hot blood of my animal-sensual nature. I have learned to be wise and cool, like my analyst. I am free of my neurotic symptoms and guilt. But is this rule of the ego truly creative? Has it furthered the process of the internalization of Eros? Has it brought me closer to the possibility of having a creative relationship? Has a transformation and humanization of my animal-sensual nature really occurred? Is the movement from instinct to archetypal idea or image (to use Jungian terminology) what we mean by internalization?

THE ANALYTICAL RITUAL

II

We can begin by attempting to arrive at some tentative conclusions regarding the last two questions. The psychic representation of the instinct, in the form of idea or image, is an essential step in the process of internalization. But it is a movement upward, a separation from the sensual-physical nature of the soul. Full internalization only occurs when the mental representation once again unites with the instinct in the centers of body consciousness. Thus a descent or return to the body is necessary. I believe this is what Jung was attempting to describe when he referred to the *unio mentalis* and *unus mundus*.[1] If this transformation process is not able to go to completion, it has the effect of increasing one's alienation from one's instinctual roots. Personality becomes increasingly narrowed instead of unfolding because the process of union between the Creative-principle (Eros) and the Pleasure-principle has been obstructed. I will attempt to describe the differences between these two stages of transformation.

For example if I feel lust for my neighbor's wife, my psychoanalytic *Weltanschaaung* allows me to give free play to these desires in the images of my fantasies without experiencing the guilt and fear I would feel were I still under the domination of the Judeo-Christian concept of sin. However it is not easy to focus on the images when I am in her presence because my emotions are intimately bound to the sexual instinct which urgently demands gratification through physical contact with the actual woman. This feat can only be accomplished if my ego is able to detach itself from the emotionally charged instinct and turn inward to focus on the psychic representations. Of course this cuts me off from any real connection with my neighbor's wife. If I am alone, it is not as dangerous to allow some of the instinctual affect to enter my consciousness along with the images. The instinct may compel me to masturbate, in which case there is no harm done. Or, more creatively, I may be able to enter into a more active relationship with my fantasies (active imagination) and gain more knowledge and

---

1. C. G. Jung, "Mysterium Coniunctionis," *CW 14*, New York: Pantheon, 1963.

understanding of the symbolic meaning contained in my illicit desires. This may have the effect of reducing the powerful instinctual need for direct physical discharge as a result of the symbolization or sublimation process. However I am not brought into a closer connection with my neighbor's wife; if anything, I now have more distance from her. My libido is now bound to the symbolic equivalent of the instinct.

Freud claimed that this sublimation of the sexual instinct is responsible for culture and humanity's creative works. Unquestionably this hypothesis contains a deep truth. Hillman, in a superb paper on the masturbation inhibition,[2] has proposed that the taboo against masturbation is archetypal, and that by preventing the immediate discharge of the sexual instinct it stimulates creative imagination activity. This is very close to Freud's view on sublimation.

The extraction, distillation, or sublimation of the psychic representation of the instinct seems to be essential for the transformation of the instincts and psychological development. The incest taboo, for example, by prohibiting immediate gratification of the incestuous desires, stimulates the production of images of the male-female union, thereby initiating the process of psychisation. Similarly, psychoanalysis stimulates and provokes the emotions and imagination, while imposing strict limitations on the spontaneous discharge of the instinctual drive within the analytical situation. Even "acting out" outside of the consulting room is viewed as a regressive fall, a sign of ego, or moral weakness which requires thorough analysis for forgiveness and redemption. The psychoanalytic model, therefore, would seem to incorporate a form which both stimulates and promotes the process of psychisation of humanity's animal instinctual nature. Where does it fail?

It fails by not only neglecting, but in actually obstructing the process of the return of the sublimated, the descent of the soul into the body. Jung, in his many references to alchemical metaphors,

---

2. James Hillman, "Towards the Archetypal Model for the Masturbation Inhibition," *Journal of Analytical Psychology* II, 1, 1966.

particularly in the *Rosarium Philosophorum* text and pictures,[3] has shown that the ascent of the sublimated soul or the Holy Spirit is followed by a descent if the process is to go to completion. The frequent failures among the practitioners of the alchemical opus probably came from a failure to complete the descent. How does this process of descent manifest itself psychologically?

Returning once again to my relationship with my neighbor's wife, I find that my psychoanalytic orientation has enabled me to reduce considerably the intensity of my instinctual-emotional drive, so that I am no longer as threatened by my erotic desires. However the Eros desire for a creative union with her, which is not identical to my sexual-sensual needs, has been neither fulfilled nor transformed. The ego cannot creatively redirect or sublimate Eros; it can only obstruct its flow, or positively, it can listen to the creative urge toward union and serve it in the best possible way. Only Eros can unite the sublimated instinct with the body. How does it feel to serve Eros?

Eros is not only responsible for internal union, but it eliminates the distance between subject and object created by the ego, thus bringing the soul into immediate contact with another. Now suppose that there has been sufficient differentiation of my sexuality so that I am no longer dominated by my sexual compulsion and can allow myself to experience my erotic desires toward my neighbor's wife while I am in her presence. I will now feel the warmth of my blood flowing toward the flesh-and-blood reality of her presence. My ego is no longer obstructing the flow of Eros, which is toward her, not inward toward a mental image. Eros has eliminated all the distance of noninvolvement and objectivity, and I feel her presence acutely in the quick of the moment, even though there has been no physical contact. My desire for physical contact is still there, but it is no longer compulsive, because Eros is joyful in having fulfilled its desire for union and the human connection. Do not devalue the fact that my Eros may be flowing toward her breasts, buttocks, or even her toe, rather than

---

3. C. G. Jung, "Psychology of the Transference," *CW 16*, New York: Pantheon, 1954.

toward the beauty of her soul or spirit or mind. The soul circulates continually throughout every cell of the body, from the highest to the lowest. I respect the wisdom of Eros, because it is like a divining-rod in its movement directly toward the quick of life.

Now if my neighbor's wife is not fearful, her soul will respond, and Eros will circulate in both directions. The soul is always aroused to unite with Eros. This is the basis of all human connection. It is, I believe, what D. H. Lawrence meant when he spoke of the "silent sexual sympathy" between male and female.[4] If the woman is open to my Eros, and I to hers, there will be a genuine flow of human warmth and tenderness between us. Still Eros is also "a mighty demon," and there is always the danger of falling into the demonic compulsiveness of an erotic love relationship when one opens oneself to Eros. What is to prevent us from falling into the very relationship we feared?

We know that the sexual instinct loses some of its compulsive character as a result of the prohibition imposed upon its immediate gratification, along with the freedom to explore its forms and imagery in fantasy. This is a fundamental step in creative psychological development. At each new phase a separation between instinct and image and a differentiation between the sensual and creative needs of the soul is necessary. But is not Eros the originator of this desire for psychological development? Does it not indicate that some of the demonic need for sexual union has already been transformed as soon as we have the desire for psychological development, and that the restraining and limiting function of Eros has to some extent already become internalized? By the time I have reached this comprehension, I need no longer fear my instinctual compulsiveness. Eros is not only urging me toward union, it is also urging me toward restraint so that each involvement can unfold as a unique and original creation. Eros desires to move from the purely erotic love connection, which demands sexual consummation, to a psychologically creative relationship in

---

4. D. H. Lawrence, "The State of Funk," *Sex, Literature and Censorship*, New York: Twayne Publishers, 1953, 66.

which union occurs on many different levels and may or may not include sexual union. We need only to listen and to trust Eros, and it will show us the way to love our neighbor's wife without violation. Eros does not speak to us from above, but from the immediacy of our emotional-bodily centers of consciousness. It restrains us mainly through anxiety, fear, and guilt, and also by closing off the soft, vulnerable opening to our soul and thereby stopping the flow toward the object of our love. But there are many other subtle and irrational feelings and intuitions through which the creative reveals itself.

How is one to know whether one is up to the demands a love will make upon us? One never really knows how much care and attention, what sacrifices love will demand, until one has submitted totally to it. So there we have a huge dilemma. One never really knows! We do know, however, that in the phenomenon of "falling in love," of "being in love," there seems to be a totality of involvement which leaves no room for anyone but the beloved. One's attention becomes totally focused on the beloved, as Ortega put it.[5] That is why it seems to be impossible to be "in love" with more than one person at a time. When one falls in love, one often neglects or betrays all former loves. It seems that the sudden and rapid influx of Eros which occurs when one falls in love is all that the human personality can handle. However, I believe it is different when one is not blinded by the passion of Cupid's arrow: that is, when one is free to choose whether or not the doors to the soul will be opened. Being in love differs from the "act of loving" in that the decision about opening oneself to love in the latter lies primarily in the hands of the individual, while in the former it is entirely in the hand of the God or Goddess, who has no limits. In "loving" one is also free to close the door, while "in love" the large gaping wound remains opened until the Deity is ready to depart. Now in answer to our question: since one never really knows what love will demand, in "loving" at least, one has the possibility of closing the door again if the demands are beyond one's capacity. But what are the effects of this opening and closing of doors?

---

5. Ortega y Gasset, *On Love*, New York: Meridian Books, 1960.

Surely the soul, which desires nothing more than to unite and mingle with another, will feel rejected and betrayed if the door once opened is closed again. On the other hand, we must not forget that the survival and integrity of the soul is dependent on the individual's capacity to carefully tend and nourish the needs of each love. I believe that it is through this process of opening and closing that the essentially impersonal Divine love begins to shape itself to fulfill the unique needs of the individual soul. This means that an open connection between two individuals cannot be sustained until Eros has transformed itself to meet the needs of the personal relationship. *It would seem that in order to be truly transformed by the impersonal Divine love, one must become involved in a long, slow, and at times painful process of transforming It.* One need not fear opening up to Love, if one does not fear closing oneself again, should its demands be beyond one's capacity to serve without destroying other loves.

For a long time I had a different image of this process of transformation through Love. I felt that it involved a slow process of opening up, of slowly removing the veils covering the naked soul, or of gradually opening the doors to one's innermost being. My experience has forced me to alter this image. I have found rather that *I am open or I am not.* When I am open it is possible for another soul to meet my soul in all its nakedness. Whether or not this occurs depends on the openness of the other and the presence of Eros. But the concept of "degrees of openness" needs correction. *One is open* or *one is not!* I believe what I have experienced as being partially or totally open is more likely owing to the duration of openness rather than the degree. Thus I have felt myself to be more or less open with someone, depending on how long I have been able to leave the door open. The image of opening and closing oneself to the circulation of Eros seems, therefore, to be not only more accurate, but if one can accept this as the "Way," one does not feel pressured to maintain the connection on a certain level. Nor does one feel guilty about closing up. Furthermore, the idea of moving toward ever deeper or higher levels of relationship then becomes secondary to the process of transforming Eros to meet the needs of the individual and personal relationship. From this point of view, the depth of the relationship would become a function of the transformation of Eros.

What conclusions can we now make concerning the psychoanalytic model? Clearly the goal of ego regulation of the instinctual-emotional life is inadequate and even obstructive to creative human relationships. Ultimately the rule of the ego must go, or one becomes cut off from the source of life. The psychoanalytic model fails because there is no possibility of completing the full humanization or transformation process, which involves the return of the sublimated to the body as it is experienced in a human relationship. Therefore a successful psychoanalysis can only lead one to an even greater alienation and detachment from one's instinctual-emotional nature and to a distortion of instinct and Eros. In spite of the fact that essential processes of transformation can occur, psychoanalysis has a dehumanizing effect, because it takes the ascent as the goal and interrupts the process at this point.

III

One would imagine, from Jung's writings, that his analytical ritual incorporates the possibility of completing the transformation process. Let us see if it does. I believe there is a basic premise in the Jungian model which is obstructive to the soul's descent into the body: namely Jung's emphasis on introversion, on the inner process as the path of individuation. His methods of becoming actively involved with the unconscious are, I believe, superior to Freud's, but they still have essentially to do with the ascent, with spiritualization, and belong, like Freud's sublimation, to what Jung himself has called the *unio mentalis.* To complete the transformation process, the *unus mundus* is needed, and on this Jung is most unclear. The *unus mundus,* or the descent of the soul into the body, can, in my opinion, be achieved only through an experience involving another person, in a process similar to that which I have attempted to describe.

Jung does go far beyond Freud in his understanding of the nature of the transference and the importance of the human connection. Jung also stresses the necessity of the analyst's human involvement and openness, the exposure of the analyst's soul to the process without the protection of the doctor's persona. This would certainly seem to be pointing in the right direction, and it is something which Freud opposed vigorously, because he felt it would be impossible for the analyst to function with the necessary objectivity and detachment. Jung, as well as Freud, realized the dangers of such openness and involvement with the patient; falling in love and becoming erotically involved being only the most obvious ones. Jung, however, seems to have found a way of avoiding the pitfalls involved in stepping out of the role of the doctor. However, I feel the Jungian claim of "humanness" in the analytical relationship is even more illusory than Freud's claim of preserving the objectivity of the doctor through his method.

I think the error in Jung's system lies in his overemphasis on the inner process. The analytical relationship is then viewed as essential primarily because a human partner is needed for the development of consciousness and psychological differentiation.[6] I think the perversity in Jungian, as well as Freudian, analysis lies in the fact that the relationship between analyst and analysand is used as a therapeutic instrument for psychological development. Eros is then continually obstructed in its desire for union with another, and redirected internally by the ego in order to effect a union with the images of its own creation. Instead of the human relationship being the opus for psychological development, as Hillman has proposed,[7] the inner process becomes the opus. What effect does this have on the human connection?

It creates a false sense of intimacy and personal involvement, a false sense of soul connection. Instead of a creative unfolding of the relationship between analyst and analysand, there is a gradual movement away from the human connection and toward intercourse with internal images.

6. Jung, "Psychology of the Transference."

THE ANALYTICAL RITUAL

Instead of the relationship becoming more human and personal, it becomes more archetypal and impersonal. I think Jungian analysts are better able to open to the heat of emotional involvement because their beliefs and concepts enable them to contain the passion of Eros. Also, because their primary concern and dedication is to the *inner process* instead of the human relationship, their egos can resist the power of Eros and rechannel its flow toward inner images. Although their method is different than the psychoanalysts, they have presumed to undertake an even more impossible task than their Freudian colleagues. Psychoanalysts, at least, acknowledge the fact that they are playing a role for the patient's benefit, but Jungians claim to be only themselves and humanly vulnerable.

To be truly human—and therefore vulnerable—one must acknowledge the soul's fundamental need to unite with another. *It is dehumanizing to use any human relationship, to use the soul's desire for connection, for any other purpose.* A true communion between two souls is a *ding an sich;* it is at once the way and the goal of the mystery of soul making. A person's relationship to one's own spirit, to one's own God, needs continual renewal and humanization through human intercourse. Without it, the creative in a person becomes a destructive anti-life force. The destructive forces which now threaten to annihilate modern humanity are, in my opinion, a result of the distortion, neglect, and devaluation of the supreme and sacred mystery of the human connection. There is no justification for using the soul's desire for union with another for a higher purpose. The soul is deeply betrayed in the analytical ritual whenever this movement toward union is misused.

The analytical model, Freudian or Jungian, in its present form at least, is anything but a paradigm for the creative relationship. However, I believe Jungian analysis, particularly, contains the potential for creating such a model.

I have proposed that in both Freudian and Jungian analysis, a considerable amount of psychisation of the animal and creative instincts is possible, but that their structures are primarily designed to promote the separation or extraction of the psychic representation

7. Hillman, "Psychological Creativity."

163

from the instinct. This phase of the process has been equated with the ascent of the soul or the *unio mentalis*. The completion of the process requires a return or descent of the soul into the body and this involves the union of the soul with another. My concern has to do with the failure of analysis to provide an adequate structure or container in which this can occur.

So long as one party is responsible for the welfare or development of the other, a psychologically creative relationship is not possible. When a patient first enters analysis, the patient has, of course, turned to the analyst for help. At this point a symmetrical relationship is neither possible nor desirable. Nevertheless the desire of the soul for union with another is behind the patient's need for help, and this will soon become manifest in the so called transference. The patient cannot be expected to cope with the powerful emotions constellated in the transference, because it is the patient's wounded Eros function which occasions the analysis in the first place. The analyst needs very much to function as the doctor, parental guide, teacher, or guru, at this point. The analyst must carry the responsibility for defining and maintaining a structure which permits a satisfactory balance between freedom and restraint. If the analyst is able to trust Eros sufficiently, the structure need not be as fixed and rigid as it is in orthodox psychoanalysis. Ultimately the analyst must be able to trust Eros; otherwise the internalization of Eros and the descent of the soul into the body is not possible. If the analyst cannot trust Eros, it means the analyst's own transformation process has become obstructed or is not completed.

To be more specific, Eros does not seem to be so desirous for the human connection during the ascending phases of analysis. It is as if "It" knows that the opus of the human connection cannot precede the opus of the inner process. The advantage of this inner regulation over externally imposed limitations is that the analyst can be truly open, spontaneous, and natural at all times. The analyst can trust any movement toward union with the analysand without fearing that a personal involvement may obstruct the process, even in the earliest phases of analysis. The analyst knows that Eros is responsible and can be trusted not to move the opus from the inner process to the human connection until the soul is sufficiently separated from the instincts to begin the return journey. So much for the ascent. We will have to discover or create a new paradigm which will promote and allow for the descent, since the current analytical models are obstructive to this process.

My description of the process, thus far, contains a fundamental fallacy. I have indicated a distinct division between the phase of ascent and descent, which is not really the way it works. Empirically, both processes go on all the time, although in the early phases of analysis, depending on the state of psychological development, the ascending phase is dominant. The psychoanalytic model functions almost entirely to promote the ascent. In order for the descent to occur, the internalization of the analyst's Eros is necessary. However it is a satisfactory internalization and humanization of the analysand's Eros that indicates that the process is completed. What is needed to ensure the possibility of this occurring? Until this occurs the analysand is not free of being dependent on the analyst for help, guidance, and healing. And not until the analyst is freed of therapeutic responsibility can the mutual desire for union and a sustained creative relationship occur.

Again this division between the completion of the descent and the beginning of a psychologically creative relationship is more theoretical than actual. The internalization of Eros is gradual, and there are moments and periods along the way during which the inequality of the doctor-patient relationship is transcended. Since I have already proposed that after the completion of the descent, the experience of a non-thera-peutic personal connection is necessary as a bridge out of the analytical ritual, I wonder now if this experience does not belong to the final stages of the descent? I suspect it does. If so this means there must be room within the analytical ritual for a *non-analytical* relationship.

In order to avoid any misunderstanding, I must clarify what I mean by *personal*. I mean by this my personal desires, needs, and feelings toward my analysand and vice versa. Do I have a need to share and live my life with him or her in the form of a true friendship? Now that I am free from the burden of therapeutic responsibility, do I still have an interest in a continuing relationship? Do I genuinely enjoy the being and presence of my analysand or has my care and concern been primarily therapeutic? Has the analysand's need for me been largely a response to my essentially impersonal, therapeutic Eros,[8] and will the analysand continue to have a need for me once the therapeutic relationship is terminated? Do the patterns of our lives move along such different paths that it would be difficult or undesirable to attempt to force a real friendship? Or, are our personalities and interests so different that we have little common ground upon which to meet aside from the analytical process? Such feelings need to be brought out into the open and resolved on a purely personal level in the final phases of the analytical ritual.

The movement from the initial archetypal constellation to a more individualized human relationship is essential to the analytical process. If it does not occur, the "wound to Eros" is more likely to be deepened rather than healed. Why should the analysand have any more trust in Eros if there is a deprivation of experiencing the trustworthiness of humanized Eros in this crucial relationship with the analyst? With even greater justification, the analysand will continue to doubt the reality of Eros as the regulating principle in human relationship.

---

8. By therapeutic Eros I mean the essentially archetypal or impesonal flow of feeling, warmth, and concern coming from the analyst toward the sick and helpless aspects of the patient's soul. It is akin to the type of protective feeling which both animals and humans seem to have toward the helpless young.

PART FIVE

Transference

"The transference phenomenon is without doubt one of the most important syndromes in the process of individuation; its wealth of meaning goes far beyond mere personal likes and dislikes."

(C. G. Jung: *The Psychology of Transference*, 1954)

"Everyone is now a stranger among strangers. Kinship libido which could still engender a satisfying feeling of belonging together, as for instance in the early Christian *communitios*—has long been deprived of its object. But, being an instinct, it is not to be satisfied by any mere substitute such as a creed, party, nation, or state. It wants the *human* connection. That is the core of the whole transference phenomenon, and it is impossible to argue it away, because relationship to the self is at once relationship to our fellow man, and no one can be related to the latter until he is related to himself."

(C. G. Jung: *The Psychology of Transference*, 1954)

CHAPTER THIRTEEN

An Archetypal View of Transference

In psychoanalysis, transference describes the phenomenon in which an individual transfers (projects) a repressed experience from the past onto a relationship in the present: i.e., the patient may experience the analyst as a critical and judgemental authority, just as he did his own father. This implies a one-sided projection from subject (patient) to object (analyst), and does not include the effects which the analyst's personality and projections have upon the relationship. The term countertransference refers only to the unconscious aspects of the analyst's psyche which are activated by the patient's transference. Patients develop transferences and analysts may develop counter-transferences in response. This is still a one-sided view which does not recognize the role which the analyst's personality plays in the formation of the transference phenomenon.

I can understand how Freud arrived at his concept of the transference. I have often enough experienced a patient, who had a cold, critical and rejecting parent, accuse me "unfairly" of treating him in the same manner: "Surely the patient must be projecting an unconscious complex onto me because I am only attempting to help him and have not done any of these things of which he accuses me." But if one examines this phenomenon in terms of every day life, then even though I may feel innocent about my patient's accusations, it does not necessarily mean that I am innocent. Such kinds of experiences occur all the time in close relationships, and rarely are the accusations totally unjust. Rather, as we have seen in our discussion of Eros, the problem most often comes from an obstruction to the connection, and when both parties have fallen into impersonal archetypal roles. I do not believe the analytical relationship is exempt from this typically human phenomenon.

The concepts of transference and projection are based on Freud's mechanistic explanations of ego development (see Introduction, p. xm): i.e., the ego attaches some of its *unformed* libido to an object and then withdraws it and the external object is introjected into the ego. Transference, in the psychoanalytic view, is seen as the obverse of this process: the object (analyst) is assumed to be unformed and a formed internal object is projected onto him.

In an archetypal theory of psychology, transference and/or projection can not occur unless the complex (archetype) is released by an appropriate stimulus. That is, whoever evokes a projection must in some way already be an incarnation of the archetype. Thus, when my patient experiences me as cold and rejecting, I must indeed be feeling and/or behaving in this way. Or, as Jung has said many times, there must always be a hook for the projection.

Both analyst and analysand are immediately thrown into the archetypal roles of Doctor-Patient, Teacher-Pupil or Parent-Child as soon as they begin working together. This is the usual initial transference constellation, but it is mutual rather than a one-sided process: the analyst projects the helpless or needy Child archetype onto the patient at the same time the patient transfers the strong, helping Father archetype onto him. As long as this continues, both parties are primarily playing out roles for each other, and the relationship is essentially impersonal.

Transference phenomena cannot be separated from the mind/body problem and the quest for inner wholeness. As long as vital portions of one's totality are not sufficiently internalized, one lives in a continual state of psychic dependency. In childhood, all the psychic functions which eventually make a child human are first experienced as belonging to others. Initiation into adulthood is primarily a process in which the archetypal projections carried by parental figures are gradually withdrawn and internalized. In our culture there has been a serious breakdown in this essential humanizing process. The phenomenon of one person becoming the carrier of an unconscious or neglected archetypal factor for another always occurs when one is powerfully drawn, by attraction or repulsion, to another person. Archetypal projection does not necessarily diminish as one comes closer to inner balance. It is probably an essential factor in any dynamically creative relationship, turning negative and obstructive only when the archetypal constellation becomes frozen. Psychic internalization is never a final thing; it is a continual, individualized path which contains the key to the mystery of man's psychological development. The parental fixations so characteristic of our culture are largely responsible for our arrested capacities to internalize. As a consequence we tend to become fixed, stuck in archetypal boxes in our most important relationships. Arrested internalization also prevents us from living our own 'child'—that is, we lose our capacity for imaginal freedom. Only as we free ourselves of the parental fixations, can *we be the child* and find our emotional imagination. Since imagination is so essential for psychological self-realization, let us briefly consider this issue before continuing our discussion of the transference.

A disturbed relationship to the imaginal world may manifest itself not only as a failure or cramp of the imagination, but also as a lack of differentiation between the inner imaginal realm and the outer concrete world. Probably both the failure of the imagination and its undifferentiatedness belong together. For example, the apparently wild, uninhibited fantasy life that occurs in many psychotic states is quite frequently a defense against painful or unacceptable emotions and fantasies. Delusional fantasies in psychosis are often a consequence of severe repression that cramps the imagination. On the other hand, those whose imagination seems sparse and obstructed often fear opening themselves to their inner images because they have no clear distinction between the inner imaginal realm of thought and feeling and the outer realm of expression and action.

Creative psychological development, individuation, is dependent on spiritual freedom. When we say someone has a free spirit do we mean that they freely or necessarily transgress the imposed manners, mores, and taboos of their culture? I think not. But it does mean the freedom to do anything or go any place they desire in the imaginal realm. They are people who have clearly distinguished the sacral, timeless world from the secular, historical world. They know they can move with unashamed dignity among the Gods and demons of the imaginal world without fear of transgressing the taboos which belong to the mundane world. Such freedom cannot occur with a primitive form of consciousness in which inner and outer reality are governed by the same laws and values. In this sense, our Judeo-Christian tradition is primitive in that thoughts and desires are subject to the same dogma, the same regulation, as deeds. Spiritual freedom requires a break with biblical tradition and the development of a new form of consciousness—a consciousness which promotes the cultivation of imaginal freedom.

Returning now to the transference, consider the ways in which it is or can be used therapeutically: as an instrument for increasing awareness and differentiation; as a possibility for experiencing certain critical archetypal constellations with the analyst; as a means of moving out of an archetypal fixation into a more individualized human relationship. This last, above all is, enormously healing. After a number of such healing experiences, the capacity to internalize begins to become a viable and reliable function, and one grows much less fearful of exposing soul to others.

From these formulations we see that the right understanding of the transference helps provide an authentic healing experience. If the transference is unconscious or misused, the best that can be hoped for is an increase in ego-consciousness and, at its worst, an increase in the mind/body split and greater distrust for open human relationships. It also becomes apparent that the important questions concerning the resolution of the transference need to be reconsidered. Since it is part of the human condition to fall continually into archetypal constellations, the idea that the transference is resolved only when all the archetypal projections are withdrawn and internalized, is a false and impossible objective. I would propose a more plausable objective for transference resolution: *the development of the capacity to internalize,*—as evidenced by the individual's ability to recognize and eventually move out of any archetypal constellations.

So long as the analytical situation continues, it will not be possible to move permanently out of the archetypal situation which forces the analyst into the role of the *carrier of greater consciousness.* Although this archetypal constellation may have been transcended, the very nature of the situation makes it inevitable that both parties fall back into it. The definite termination of the analytical relationship is essential if one is to get out of this archetypal box. But termination is difficult because it generally means a termination of a relationship which may have become important as a thing in itself, aside from its therapeutic or spiritual goals. The possibility of a vessel for a continued relationship must be there or the relationship will become stuck in an archetypal situation where the analyst carries greater consciousness, whether or not the analysis continues or breaks off. Freud and Jung's seminars and Jung's club, which his analysands could join, were perhaps attempts to meet this need for some form in which the connection could be continued. This structure has in recent years moved toward a therapeutic group experience. One objection to these forms is that the analyst still ends up in the archetypal role of the carrier of consciousness, and there is no possibility of analyst and analysand realizing the individualized dimension of their relationship, its value, meaning, and place in the larger pattern of their lives.

Why is such a realization essential for the analytical process and the resolution of the transference? Is it not enough for the patient to have developed the capacity to internalize? Yes, that would be enough, but still the possibility of experiencing a more personal relationship is essential for both analyst and analysand or the internalizing function becomes hollow and meaningless. If internalization is experienced as an end to a deeply meaningful human connection, who wants it? When children or adolescents become stuck in a parental fixation, it is not necessarily because they are unable to get out of it, but as often as not they fear that if they get out of the archetypal role, they will be cut off from the warm and positive human things so important to soul. If analysis repeats this wounding parent-child archetypal experience, the patient ends up with the same sense of disillusionment and betrayal as does the child.

A sense of the inner child suffering from wounding love relationships is usually what brings a person into analysis. As a result of those childhood wounds to the soul, the Eros function is generally undeveloped or damaged. This makes it extremely difficult, if not impossible, for one to experience an intimate and creatively evolving human connection. In this sense the wounded child also represents that aspect of the soul which needs and demands union with another. The analyst's compassion and desire to help this child constellates the fundamental human need for union, and the desire for union between analyst and analysand is set in motion. But the Eros development of the child alone is not sufficient to enable it to enter into union. The child is primarily dependent on the other's love. Therefore an analyst's Eros connection with the wounded child, and the desire to help it, initiates the positive transference.

Nevertheless, patients are not children. Unless they have been too severely damaged, patients are generally capable of experiencing adult passion and desire for union. Although it is generally the wounded child which evokes the analyst's love, the consequent flow of love involves the totality of both analyst and analysand. Eros circulates not only around the inner child, but also between the two people involved with its care. Thus, while the transference is of the nature of the parent-child relationship, it also includes the ingredients of an adult love and friendship. However there is no possibility for fulfilling the soul's desire for union until the child is transformed and healed. Its neglected and abused nature must be attended to before it becomes capable of loving another.

This contamination of the instinctual needs of the sick, neglected child and the soul's need to love another is a primary source of the difficulties arising in the analytical relationship. That the child experiences the analyst as father, mother, healing God, etc., does not take away from the fact that the flow of love has been set in motion. It is vital for both analyst and analysand to maintain the Eros connection, and whenever it is obstructed or cut off (most frequently because of the demands of the child) it is the child in need of healing who suffers most. But the soul in each of the participants also suffers because of its desire for union.

The mutual need of analyst and analysand for soul-connection is behind the entangling archetypal projections released in the transference. All attempts to further the psychological development of the patient, all attempts to understand and eliminate the obstructive resistances and other manifestations of the negative transference, are only partially due to the therapeutic concern and desire of the analyst. The deepest need of the soul in any human relationship is never therapeutic; it is the desire to unite with the other. Thus, the analyst's desire to heal is never pure. Even when the analyst attempts to assume an objective scientific stance, attempting to focus on the wound or psychopathology, the flow of Eros is set in motion and this activates the analyst's need for human connection.

The capacity of both analyst and analysand to sustain the Eros connection to the wounded child is largely dependent on the flow between them. A differentiation between the love for each other and for the child is artificial to some extent, but it is a necessary one to make. The parallel might be seen in the relationship of a husband and wife, when both are concerned with promoting the child's health and development. The love between parent and child, however, is largely one-sided, because the child's Eros is undeveloped and largely bound to its basic instinctual needs. A mutual desire and capacity for communion is needed or the equality of a creative relationship is not possible. Psychologically we know how important is the Parents' connection with each other and how important to the welfare of the child, can be the consequences of their lack of connection. When the connection is absent, the child becomes burdened with the unfulfilled need for communion of the mother or father, at the expense of its own development.

When the need for union between analyst and analysand is given less value than the therapeutic need of the relationship, this need for union will function autonomously and unconsciously just as it does in the typical negative parent-child relationship. Instead of the neglected child being healed in analysis, its wound will be further deepened. Moreover, by calling the need for union "transference" and attempting to interpret it (away), therapy becomes the destructive reverse of itself. Both the child and the soul's individuation are damaged.

THE NEGATIVE TRANSFERENCE

The emotional frustration and disillusionment which the child experienced in relationship to the parent is reconstellated in the negative transference. This aspect of the analytical relationship must be resolved satisfactorily; if it isn't, the internal union between the masculine and feminine opposites does not occur. This experience is an essential step in the process of reestablishing a connection with one's soul.

The demands of the wounded child are largely responsible for the soul-splitting fixation which occurs in the negative transference. But, as we have seen, the child is wounded primarily because vital parts of its soul were not internalized and continued to be carried by parental figures. The patient initially experiences this lost part of soul as belonging to the analyst. Much of the frustration and anger which follows comes from an inability to unite with this image which the analyst has incarnated. Since no such union is possible, acceptance of this reality is the only healing solution to the negative transference. The patients' need for union with their own soul is behind this idealized image. This phenomenon should be elaborated further.

AN ARCHETYPAL VIEW OF TRANSFERENCE

The negative parental experience occurs when the child must carry vital aspects of a parent's soul, generally the consequence of lack of soul-connection between husband and wife. The typical incestuous triangle results and the child is robbed of the possibility of experiencing its totality in relationship to either parent. Instead of experiencing the basic attraction and harmony between the masculine and feminine opposites, the child experiences these archetypes—yang and yin, sun and moon, heaven and earth, and spirit and flesh as hostile opponents. This above all seems responsible for the mind/body split which afflicts modern man. The desperate need to heal this split, to become whole, is at the core of the negative transference. Whether it is the mother or father archetype or the hero-saviour-lover archetype that constellates in the transference, still it is the need for the unification of the archetypal King and Queen, the *hierosgamos,* which is behind transference. Not until harmony is restored to the *internal* masculine/feminine opposites can a soul-connection be maintained. Analytical transference is resolved once there is a full acceptance on the part of both analyst and analysand that the fulfillment of this archetypal need in their relationship is neither possible nor desirable.

The nature of this mutually frustrating aspect of the analytical relationship needs to be understood and accepted before termination. If this does not occur, both parties end the analysis with the delusion that all is right and good between them. Such a delusion tends to perpetuate the internal split within the patient because he has not really been confronted with the impossibility of the archetypal situation. Since the soul's frustration in the negative transference is identical to the child's incestuous entanglement with the negative parent, this wounding experience of childhood is only repeated if analysis ends with the false premise that analyst and analysand are pleased by their connection with each other. Of course, it is also wounding when the patient terminates analysis with anger and disillusionment. There must be a mutual understanding and respect for the frustrating archetypal situation which analysis constellates. This recognition of the essentially *impersonal* nature of the obstructions which are interfering with soul-connection humanizes, and it is then possible to terminate with dignity, mutual respect, and positive personal feelings, free of soul-splitting delusion. The idea that the negative transference can be changed within the analytical situation is danger-ous and misleading. It tends to prolong greatly the analytical relationship. And the enormous value of terminating analysis with the negative transference still intact and out in the open is completely lost. To recapitulate: the full mutual acceptance of the negative transference promotes the internal reconciliation of the masculine and feminine opposites. This internalization of the archetypes of union (the incest archetype) is the key to soul-connection and individuation.

There is still another dimension to the transference dilemma. Especially in Jungian analysis, the analytical experience is often equivalent to being initiated into a spiritual order or mystery cult. The profound changes that occur constellate kinship libido, which then understandably tends to move toward other initiates. If one has experienced an authentic rebirth, one is ready to enter into a new life where kinship of spirit becomes a stronger bond than kinship of blood. It has been my experience that unless spiritual kinship develops between analyst and analysand, the process is too limited. This kinship connection is a bond which does not break with the termi-nation of analysis. It can be destroyed, however, if the negative transference is not accepted, or consequently, if there is a denial of the validity of the analytical experience. The lack of firmly rooted kinship connections is perhaps more responsible for modern man's sense of isolation and alienation than any other single factor. Frequent renewal through kinship connections is basic nourishment for man's spiritual and physical well-being.

TRANSFERENCE AND INNER WHOLENESS

The splitting of the atom corresponds to a similar phenomenon within the soul of a person. Tremendous forces of potential destruc-tion have been unleashed in the material and spiritual worlds as a result of this apparent accomplishment. Much of the anxiety, fear, and despair of modern humanity is a consequence of this long and slowly evolving historical process; a process in which the rational portion or a person's soul has become progressively separated and split off from the greater totality of being, finally reaching its present disembodied state. In this disembodied state it has become capable of the type of cool scientific objectivity which has allowed humanity to create nuclear weapons and many other mechanized scientific achievements which threaten to annihilate their creator.

The energy released as a result of this fission of the atom and the soul, has set off a chain reaction of increasing fragmentation. However, the vision of wholeness, of internal union, of warmblooded connections to others and to the cosmos, has not been lost. People know that they have lost connection with the vital life-giving centers of their own being and their life-renewing connections with others. This is both the source of hope and of a restless dissatisfaction and despair. How can a person regain an essential wholeness and reconnect a rational mind to an incarnated soul? How can a person heal the painful wound of the split atom?

The physical scientists have been working toward releasing energy more creatively through atomic fusion instead of fission. And psychotherapy, in spite of its many failures and shortcomings, is moving away from its emphasis on consciousness toward the problem of humanity's isolation and alienation. But we are still a long way off from any real solution to our modern physical and spiritual dilemma; and there is no assurance that we shall succeed. One danger lies in the tendency to seek societal solutions to a problem which arises primarily from the split within the individual soul. Not that collective efforts are not also needed, but they are doomed to failure if they are made at the expense of the soul. Hope, therefore, lies mainly in our capacity to achieve individual psychic wholeness.

The trend toward experiencing wholeness through connections to others, through group encounters, and communal identification, misses an important point. As healing as such experiences may be, they are at best temporary because one does not necessarily move

closer to an internal union. The reaction against individual psychotherapy, even though it is perhaps warranted, threatens to lead us away
from a therapeutic ritual which has a greater potential than the group
experience for effecting significant healing of the mind/body split.

When the soul is split there is always a persistent need and
longing, consciously or unconsciously, for reunion. This is most
often experienced as a feeling of having lost something vital and
precious. We may have either vague or sharp memories of having,
somewhere in childhood or in the past or in another life, experienced
the warm and sensual throbbings of this mysterious essence of
life; we feel incomplete and empty without it. Our longing to regain
the sense of well-being and wholeness leads us down many paths.
Naturally, we seek outside ourselves for this lost portion of our soul
because we have no idea at first that it is lying deeply within the
center of our own being. We tend to catch fleeting glimpses of this
elusive soul-substance in our encounters with others, and when we
fall "in love" we feel we have at last found it. Above all, we become
largely dependent on our connections with other human beings for
our own sense of wholeness. Whoever carries for us this vital portion
of our lost soul is capable of wounding us deeply, of destroying our
sense of self worth, wholeness and meaning. And such people will
continually fail and betray us, because no one can live up to the image
of our own soul. This awareness tends to make us progressively more
cautious and reticent about exposing and expressing our own needs,
desires and love for others; which only increases our internal split
and sense of isolation.

Because of the nature of the analytical vessel and the genuine
concern of the analyst, the neglected, abandoned soul begins to stir
and move out of its hidden chamber. A great flow of warmth and
feeling goes toward the analyst, who is soon experienced as possessing
and containing the mysterious substance which one needs for
completion. This has been described as being due to the phenomenon
of projection. It is an effectively working concept, though incomplete;
I believe it is also owing to the experience of soul which is encouraged

180

and desired in the analytical situation. Be that as it may, this experience of one's lost soul, in a therapeutic situation, offers the possibility of ultimately regaining it. From this point of view, it becomes clear that the relationship to the analyst is central to this process of reintegrating and reuniting with one's own soul.

Having discussed the nature and importance of the analyst-patient relationship, I want to emphasize inner union as the ultimate goal of analysis, rather than union with another. We have seen how the inner and outer connection go hand in hand, but a further differentiation is needed.

The emotion of love is the essential stuff of internal union as well as union with another. Inner wholeness cannot be maintained for long if there is a disturbance of the Eros function. *So long as one fears loving and exposing one's soul to another, internal union is not possible.* Thus, the goal of inner wholeness, in analysis, cannot be achieved so long as the obstacles to a totally open connection between analyst and analysand continue to exist. On the other hand, an unobstructed channel does not necessarily mean that a firm bond of inner connectedness has been established. As long as the analyst is the carrier of a portion of the patient's soul (and vice versa), the state of inner wholeness is constantly in jeopardy. This stage of the process is perhaps the most difficult, when and if it is ever reached. It is the place where many potentially successful analyses fail.

Paradoxically, the experience of an unobstructed flow and connection, the very experience of one's wholeness in relationship to the analyst, is at the heart of the problem. In order to understand this, we need to say more about the peculiar nature of the analytical vessel. There are few viable vessels or containers for human relationship in our Western culture, where two individuals meet together regularly for the specific purpose of cultivating soul. The containers for human relationship in our culture, including marriage in its present state, do anything but promote wholeness of connection. Both analyst and analysand, therefore, must face the fact that they will probably not be able to sustain as unobstructed a connection in their "worldly" relationships as they have had in their analytical relationship. How-ever, the analyst is confronted with another difficulty: this involves the explicit or implicit promise that the positive connection to the analyst will ultimately be replaced by equally deep and open connections to others in the world. One can see that this promise is not so easily kept.

Moving into the final stage of analysis would seem, therefore, to necessitate the full and mutual recognition of the special unworldly nature of the analytical vessel and relationship. Both analyst and patient must be able to recognize their need, if it exists, to continue the relatively unobstructed relationship they have with each other and the impossibility of doing so. The conscious sacrifice they must make is similar to that which both a parent and child must make when the child is ready to leave the containment of the parental fold and enter the world. In a positive parent-child relationship, of which there are few nowadays, the child has no assurance that he will ever feel as closely connected to another as he has been to his parent. Yet the child must go and the parent must encourage him to leave. Of course, the situation is not identical in analysis; but it is a bitter pill to swallow when one realizes it is going to be extremely difficult to find or create a comparable vessel in everyday life which cultivates soul-connection and soul-transformation. If the patient is unable to fully accept and appreciate this reality, if one feels betrayed and disillusioned by it, the wound to the soul will remain unhealed. And if the analyst has a similar difficulty, the analyst will experience a sense of failure and ultimate disillusionment with analysis.

The importance of viable creative vessels for the promotion of soul connection cannot be overemphasized. These vessels are the basic social forms and structures of society. They influence and determine the life patterns and life-style of a culture. There is a great need nowadays for new forms in marriage, friendship and community which will promote the development of Eros and feelings of kinship connection. But it will probably be a long, long time before there will be any real creative change in the basic structural units of our society.

What are we to do, in the meantime, about the great disparity between the reality of living in a sick and fragmented world and our vision of a better way of life? What is the patient who has completed analysis to do now that he has reconnected with his soul's creative vision? Now that he has experienced the concrete reality of an open and *sustained* connection to another?

The exchange of soul-substance which occurs when two souls meet and touch, is essential for the life and health of the body and spirit. Inner wholeness soon becomes cold, rigid and life-killing if the soul is not continually re-humanized and renewed through the human connection. Still, it is just because soul-connections are so rare and difficult to have in our culture, that the internal healing of the mind/body split and internal wholeness is so essential. This is another paradox which we cannot avoid.

The need to keep one's soul carefully hidden and protected disappears when one is no longer dependent on the connection to another for completion. There is no longer the fear of experiencing and expressing one's feelings, one's reactions to another, simply because the integrity and wholeness of one's being are not dependent on a particular relationship. This increases the possibility of having close human connections, and it decreases the demands and expectations which we are all prone to make upon those we care for. In addition, the revealed soul generally evokes the emotion of love, especially when it demands nothing from the other. Thus, inner wholeness opens the door to many more possibilities for soul-connection, in spite of the lack of Eros promoting vessels in our culture.

But there is still another difficulty which continually threatens to undermine inner wholeness: the vision of a new and better world. Regardless of the innumerable forms this vision may take, it has its origins in the archetype of union, expressed in such images as the Brother-Sister Incest, the Heavenly or Divine Marriage, the Quaternity, the Mandala. As we have seen, a connection to this archetype and the belief that it will eventually be fulfilled, gives direction, meaning and balance to life. Realization and fulfillment can occur on many levels internally, as inner harmony and union; externally, as union and oneness with another, the community, the world, the cosmos. The images of an ideal world through which the archetype expresses itself have certain common characteristics: namely, a world in which peace, harmony and brotherly love are the rule; a kinship community in which each man moves with proud and quiet dignity protected from invasion by alien forces; a community ruled by the Eros principle, where the aggressive instincts and the power principle are working creatively for truth, beauty and aesthetic values. These elements are the common ground upon which all utopian visions of an earthly paradise, a New Jerusalem, are based.

Perhaps in the Golden Age, or before the Fall, humanity did realize and fulfill this vision; perhaps there have been communities throughout history which have approximated it. We are now living in a period which seems a polar opposite to the Utopian vision, in spite of all our material affluence. The faith that the Utopian vision will one day be realized is, now more than ever, essential in order to maintain one's balance and sanity. Any realistic appraisal of existing conditions and the forces at work, however, can only fill one with a deep despair about the future. How can one hold onto the belief that a better world is possible in the face of the hard facts? How is one to realize any joy and meaning in daily life, living as we do in this fragmented and fragmenting world? Dropping out and attempting to create a new and viable community never seems to work for long. Confronted with the impossibility of escaping the fate of all modern men, it is extremely difficult to maintain one's faith and connection to the Utopian vision. Inner harmony and wholeness of being begin to crumble whenever we lose faith in this vision. Analysis must be able to show the individual an effective way of maintaining his faith in the ultimate fulfillment of his Utopian vision, in spite of the hard and cruel facts of reality, or it will fail in its promise to guide the individual along the path of self-realization and wholeness.

CHAPTER FOURTEEN

Beyond Transference: A New Analysis

A lthough the capacity to internalize is a more plausible therapeutic objective than the resolution of the transference, I believe
an even more radical departure from orthodox views is needed:
the use of the transference phenomenon as a *therapeutic instrument is*
unnecessary and, moreover, even detrimental to the human connection.

If I attempt to tell another person where he or she is psychologically in relationship to me, in or out of analysis, I cut off the flow of
connection between us. The validity of what I have to say about what
is going on inside another is always questionable. I can say no more
about my relationship to another than what I myself experience. To
attempt to tell another how he or she is experiencing me is a bit of
destructive scientific hubris. My psychological knowledge may give
me some insight into what is happening between us, but it is impossible to be sure of what belongs to me and what belongs to the other.
Furthermore it is destructive to a relationship for one person to detach
and attempt to make an impersonal judgement about what is going on
between them. The use of transference as a therapeutic instrument is
bad for soul. It promotes a continuing dependency on the analyst,
working against the individuation process and tending to make the
analytical ritual interminable.

A patient can become aware of the projections occurring in the
analytical relationship without the transference being interpreted. If
the analyst is willing to expose feelings in the relationship, this, more
than anything else, helps the analysand to differentiate between
fantasies and what is actually happening between them. Knowledge

of the transference phenomenon is essential for psychological development, but it is obstructive to the individuation process to use this knowledge as an instrument for therapy. Once one becomes sensitive to what is going on *inside,* a person can discover within all the insight needed to understand the dynamics of the relationship.

The goal of the analytical process can be simply stated—soul-connection—a right relationship between ego and soul. Once an individual is engaged with this goal and can follow the path of individuation, the analysis is best terminated as soon as possible. After all, a person is born individuated and one's development depends on maintaining this state through a dynamic dialectical ego-soul relationship. The ideas that individuation is a heroic and difficult quest for a treasure, that it involves a progressive overcoming of obstacles, or the mystical union with God, are insidious and perpetuate a continued dependency on the analyst. For modern humanity the hero myth is no longer an adequate paradigm. We need a new paradigm which promotes soul-connection instead of the hero's insatiable drive toward knowledge, power, and consciousness.

A more effective approach to the healing of the incest wound certainly would have to be incorporated into a new analysis. Some steps which need to be emphasized are as follows:

1) Since the humanization of Eros is dependent on a firm connection to the incest archetype, as is the gradual lessening of one's dependency on another for psychological completion, some understanding of this symbol is needed.

2) The incest wound manifests itself through a split between mind and body, thinking and feeling, love and sex, spirit and nature as a consequence of attempting to control personality with the rational mind. Becoming conscious of all those experiences in which one is fearful of losing rational control, of being overwhelmed by spontaneous irrational impulses and desires, is probably the best way of recognizing the wound. The first step in the healing process is the recognition of this fear as it manifests itself in a variety of relationships and experiences.

3) Exploring the origins and nature of these fears is the next step. At the same time one must begin to cultivate a greater awareness of the irrational movements of the soul as it circulates throughout the body. Finally, one must gain the courage to allow this spontaneous living pulse free expression without any opposition from the rational mind; the ego must ultimately relinquish its control and surrender to the essentially unknown, unpredictable directing intelligence within the soul. Regaining a trust in the spontaneous expressions of one's nature requires practice. It is hoped the new analysis will offer a relatively safe container in which one can gradually gain experience and trust in soul directed human interaction.

4) While individual analysis offers the above possibility, it does not offer a container for expressing and experiencing oneself with peers and in relationship to groups—one must ultimately be able to act and live out of this new center in every aspect of one's life. A more total concept of healing should include such a possibility.

5) Paradoxically the fear of being open and spontaneous, the fear of losing ego control, is often greatest in marriage. This is largely because the archetypal parent-child constellation tends to dominate modern marriages. Therefore most couples are in a childlike state of extreme dependency on each other, consciously or unconsciously. This is intensified by the isolation most couples experience because of a lack of connection to any viable kinship community. It takes more courage than most couples have to risk breaking this essentially impersonal relationship by allowing a free interchange of personal feelings and emotions to occur. A therapeutic situation which promotes a more spontaneous direct interchange between husband and wife must therefore be available in the new analysis. How can one speak of any real healing of the incest wound if the marriage relationship is still fragmented?

6) The non-therapeutic experience of working together with others who are also attempting to act out of their soul-centers rather than their ego-centers offers the possibility of establishing an authentic kinship community. There can be no permanent healing of the incest

187

wound unless one feels rooted in a community. The vitality of the individual male-female connection is soon killed if a couple is cut off from a kinship community—the demands of the basically impersonal kinship libido become an overwhelming burden to the development of a personal relationship.

In a new analysis most of the existing methods of promoting soul connection could be retained: dreams, active imagination and imaginative activity, becoming aware of what one is feeling and experiencing in relationships, learning to appreciate the symbolic language of the psyche and some, and learning to differentiate between inner and outer reality. In addition, groups which will stimulate an open exchange of feelings and ideas need to be incorporated into the approach. The lack of group experience is an unfortunate omission in orthodox analysis. Many individuals need to be approached from this vantage point before they can begin to internalize their projections.

The difficulties which one encounters internally in relationship to the soul are clearly manifested externally in relationship with others, particularly with the opposite sex. Consequently, it is delusional to assume that fundamental internal changes have occurred as long as the pattern of relationship with the opposite sex is essentially unchanged. In individual therapy there is no way for the analyst to observe the analysand in an actual encounter with someone else. Is such a vantage point necessary? Orthodox analysts would say "no," that these same patterns occur and can be observed within the transference situation. A new analysis will not be able to make such a claim, even if it were valid, since the transference will no longer be used as a therapeutic instrument.

We can much more clearly see where two people are caught with each other when we are not entangled in their involvement. The analyst's knowledge of archetypal patterns can be used most creatively with the opportunity to see the analysand in actual encounter with another. At times the repeated chopping away at these archetypal patterns, as they become manifest in actual relationship, is the only thing that will enable the analysand to move to a new relationship with the soul.

BEYOND TRANSFERENCE: A NEW ANALYSIS

The major methodological and structural changes in a new analysis may be summarized as follows:

1) Elimination of the therapeutic use of the transference phenomenon.

2) Cultivation of mutual openness: experiencing and expressing what one is thinking, feeling, and fantasizing in relationship with the other. Both parties would feel free to express their experience of the other without fear of breaking the relationship should such expressions be disturbing or hurtful.

3) With the elimination of the use of the transference, there is no justification for anyone becoming dependent on a particular therapist. No therapist can use on the patient the old ploy of "working through" the transference or working through anything. The notion of resolving a complex is based on a medical model of analysis. A new analysis makes no claim to cure or resolve a neurotic complex. It claims only to help the individual in relationship with soul through a process which is essentially educational.

In traditional analytical systems process is understood as a systematic working through and integration of psychological complexes. Process in the new analysis is viewed in terms of changing attitudes, of changing modes of perceiving inner and outer reality. Integration of complexes is not the nature of the process but a consequence of being in process. Simply put, the movement from an ego-centered to a soul-centered view of reality is what being-in-process means.

4) The idea of working with only one analyst at a time originates from the emphasis on transference and working through a complex. With these theoretical objections out of the way, a simultaneous therapeutic experience with several analysts could become a part of the ritual.

5) Some form of therapeutically educational group experience needs to be incorporated into this new analysis.

6) A permanent forum is needed for the exchange of ideas about individuation as both a personal and societal problem. Such a forum offers an essential meeting ground for a spiritual kinship community.

7) Since analyzing psychic phenomena and complexes is no longer central in the new analysis, a more appropriate name is needed. Why not follow Hillman's suggestion and call it Archetypal Psychology[1] or Archetypal Therapy? Further archetypal therapy is not rooted in either modern medicine or academic psychology; rather, it belongs in the tradition of those educational, spiritual, and religious disciplines concerned with the life of the soul.

Whenever I am able to step outside my profession and view it from a distance, I am appalled by the insanity of the analytical relationship. What an abomination to call what goes on within the orthodox analytical structure a relationship! How can two people connect to each other, be themselves with each other, if they are not free to become emotionally involved or have physical contact with each other?

Most of the transference difficulties are created and perpetuated by the soul's frustration in not being able to have a relationship with the analyst. While the psychoanalytic ritual has been a fantastic laboratory for examining the pathologies of human relationships, an analyzed person is not necessarily more open or loving. On the contrary, analysands tend to follow the example of their analyst in dealing with irrational impulses and emotions. The identity of the analyst and how that analyst reacts as a person is therefore the most determining aspect of the therapeutic experience. But the analyst is trained to be a nonperson: detached, objective, and uninvolved. Incredible! Could there possibly be a worse model for promoting the human connection?

To demand that the therapist remain detached and emotionally uninvolved is not only unrealistic, but inhuman and harmful to the soul of both patient and therapist; in addition it recreates the wounding pathogenic parent-child relationship (pathogenic parents are threatened by emotional involvement with the child and are fearful of being natural and spontaneous). These incestuous wounds interfere

---

1. James Hillman, "Why 'Archetypal' Psychology?" in *Spirng 1970*, Spring Publications: New York, 1970.

with the individual's capacity for intimate human relationships, and they tend to create an internal split between one's spiritual and animal instinctual natures. The therapist must be open to experiencing emotional closeness with the patient in order to promote the healing of these wounds; this is not possible so long as either or both parties fear their bodily reactions and sexuality. Overcoming this fear and gaining the trust to express what is going on emotionally, bodily, and imaginally in the relationship, is an essential part of the therapeutic process.

Will such mutual openness not tend to provoke concrete sexual involvement? In my experience this has not been the case; quite the contrary. The less open and connected people are with each other, the more they seem to feel compelled to act on their sexual impulses in order to make a connection. Most of the sexuality which goes on nowadays has this compulsive quality, just because there is so little Eros and connection between people.

Without Eros there can be no real connection between people. When Eros flows, mind and body are in harmony. Whenever one experiences a conflict between these opposites in a relationship, it means Eros is obstructed. To attempt to break through the obstruction by acting upon the sexual desire, for example, tends to sever the connection and create even more distance between people. Thus overcoming one's sexual inhibitions and becoming sexually free does not necessarily lead to better or healthier sex. Without Eros there is no possibility for good sex.

In this book I have emphasized the central importance of getting right with one's sexuality so that one can be spontaneous and trusting of all instincts. But the new sexual freedom which soul needs has less to do with action than with emotional and imaginal realization. I do not mean to put down the new freedom to act out the full range of one's sexual impulses and fantasies without moral condemnation. But I think it does miss the point a bit, as do the new sex therapies. D. H. Lawrence understood all this better than any other modern writer or psychologist I know:

Far be it from me to suggest that all women should go running after gamekeepers for lovers. Far be it from me to suggest that they should be running after anybody. A great many men and women today are happiest when they abstain and stay sexually apart, quite clean and at the same time, when they understand and realize sex more fully. Ours is the day of realization rather than action. There has been so much action in the past, especially sexual action, a wearying repetition over and over, without a corresponding thought, a corresponding realization. Now our business is to realize sex. *Today the full conscious realization of sex is even more important than the act itself.* After centuries of obfuscation, the mind demands to know and know fully. The body is a good deal in abeyance, really. When people act in sex, nowadays, they are half the time acting up. They do it because they think it is expected of them. Whereas as a matter of fact *it is the mind which is interested, and the body has to be provoked* The reason being that our ancestors have so assiduously acted sex without ever thinking it or realizing it, that now the act tends to be mechanical, dull and disappointing, and only fresh mental realization will freshen up the experience.

The mind has to catch up, in sex: indeed, in all the physical acts. Mentally, we lag behind in our sexual thought, in a dimness, a lurking, grovelling fear which belongs to our raw, somewhat bestial ancestors. In this one respect, sexual and physical, we have left the mind unevolved. Now we have to catch up, and make a balance between the consciousness of the body's sensations and experiences, and these sensations and experiences themselves. *Balance up the consciousness of the act, and the act itself. Get the two in harmony.* It means having a proper reverence for sex, and a proper awe of the body's strange experience . . .[2] (my italics)

I have revealed the enormous difficulties I had in even allowing my erotic feelings and fantasies to enter consciousness. Exposing this material in the therapeutic situation was even more difficult. Nevertheless my convictions about the fragmenting effects of the archetypal

---

2. D. H. Lawrence, "A Propos of Lady Chatterley's Lover," in *Sex, Literature and Censorship,* New York: Twayne Publishers, 1953, 92-93.

analyst-analysand relationship gave me the courage to risk such exposure. It was a gradual process, filled with pitfalls, and I made many painful, but probably necessary, blunders in my attempts to pursue this uncharted course. One of the pitfalls was actual erotic involvement, which occurred just because I was still too fearful of allowing my sexual feelings and fantasies to enter full consciousness. Since the conscious tension between mind/body, spirit/flesh, love/sex is essential to the therapeutic process, surrender to sensuality tends to put an end to the therapeutic nature of the relationship.

On principle, therefore, I do not recommend sexual involvement in the psychotherapeutic situation, yet I doubt that young psychotherapists can learn to trust Eros and the sexual instinct if they are unable to risk this possibility. It is a danger well worth the risk. Better to be humanly vulnerable than perpetuate the dehumanizing archetypal situation of classical analysis. On the other hand as long as therapists are working within the prevailing medical model, should they become sexually involved in the therapeutic situation, they will feel either that they have committed an horrendous crime, or they may attempt to justify it as being "therapeutic."

Clearly analysis must be free of the limitations of the psychoanalytic medical model if the roles of doctor and patient are to be transcended. All of the presumptions of this model concerning emotional involvement, physical contact, regularity of meeting, payment of fee, etc., need to be reexamined. As long as the analytical relationship remains stuck in an archetypal box, no real healing of the incest wound can occur, and the individual continues to remain bound to his parental complexes. How can analysis claim therapeutic efficacy if the Eros obstructing effects of the incest wound remain essentially unchanged or deepened? Even if the expansion of consciousness rather than healing is taken as the goal, one must question the value of an increase in consciousness which does not promote the development of Eros.

Fortunately the humanity of most analysts cannot tolerate the antihuman structure of the psychoanalytic model; unquestionably, much more emotional involvement and physical contact goes on than is revealed in professional papers. Even if the analyst has difficulty getting out of an archetypal role, the struggle to be more open and personally connected helps to humanize the relationship. While some healing may occur with such an analyst, it is still inadequate. Not until both parties can face each other without any of the protective structural barriers, each responsible for their own feelings and actions (and only their own), can the archetypal pattern be broken. Why, then, is there so much fear among psychotherapists of discarding the psychoanalytic model?

Psychoanalysis originated out of Freud's interest in hysteria, and most of his early patients were hysterical women. No doubt he had to protect himself against these irrational, demanding, emotionally-charged women. What better way to do it than to establish the dogma of the psychoanalytic ground rules?

Freud was brave in being among the first to try to listen with sympathetic understanding to the agony and dark passions of the suffering hysterical female. He deserved all the protection he could find because exposure to the wrath of the injured Goddess (archetype) is fraught with danger (the relationship between hysteria and the bisexual Dionysus, who is mainly a god of women, has been developed in great detail by Hillman in his essay, *On Psychological Femininity*).[3] Because Freud and his followers needed these protective measures does not necessarily mean that they are now essential, or that they are good for the patient. In this book I have, in fact, presented considerable evidence to the contrary. More and more the psychoanalytic structure begins to look like a masculine defense against dark feminine nature. To allow the Goddess or Dionysus an equal say and equal rights is much too threatening to our hypertrophied Apollonian consciousness. Besides, is it not all for a woman's own good that a therapist maintain an Apollonian distance and objectivity? Who's good? Is this not another blatant example of chauvinism? Can the analysand (male or female) ever feel anything

---

3. James Hillman, "On Psychological Feminity," in *The Myth of Analysis*, Evanston, Ill.: Northwestern UP, 1972.

but childlike and inferior as long as the analyst assumes responsibility for protecting both of them from the spontaneous involving tendencies of Eros?

A new model for the analytical ritual must above all recognize the central importance of the relationship (not transference) between analyst and analysand. Eros development through the cultivation of soul connection is the new goal of the *process* rather than self-knowledge and the expansion of consciousness, even though the former cannot occur without the latter. The goal of the *relationship* is to move from the initial archetypal parent-child constellation to one of equality and personal involvement. The goal of the process and the goal of the relationship go hand in hand, so that one cannot be reached without the other. Thus, when the relationship becomes truly personal and individualized, this is an indication that the therapeutic ritual is nearing its goal.